An apology for Christianity, in a series of letters, addressed to Edward Gibbon, ... By R. Watson, ... Fifth edition.

Richard Watson

ECCO
PRINT EDITIONS

An apology for Christianity, in a series of letters, addressed to Edward Gibbon, ... By R. Watson, ... Fifth edition.
Watson, Richard
ESTCID: T075719
Reproduction from British Library
With a half-title.
London : printed for T. Evans; J. and J. Merrill, Cambridge; J. Fletcher, and Prince and Cooke, Oxford; P. Hill, Edinburgh; and W. M'Kenzie, Dublin, 1791.
vii,[1],250p. ; 12°

Eighteenth Century
Collections Online
Print Editions

Gale ECCO Print Editions

Relive history with *Eighteenth Century Collections Online*, now available in print for the independent historian and collector. This series includes the most significant English-language and foreign-language works printed in Great Britain during the eighteenth century, and is organized in seven different subject areas including literature and language; medicine, science, and technology; and religion and philosophy. The collection also includes thousands of important works from the Americas.

The eighteenth century has been called "The Age of Enlightenment." It was a period of rapid advance in print culture and publishing, in world exploration, and in the rapid growth of science and technology – all of which had a profound impact on the political and cultural landscape. At the end of the century the American Revolution, French Revolution and Industrial Revolution, perhaps three of the most significant events in modern history, set in motion developments that eventually dominated world political, economic, and social life.

In a groundbreaking effort, Gale initiated a revolution of its own: digitization of epic proportions to preserve these invaluable works in the largest online archive of its kind. Contributions from major world libraries constitute over 175,000 original printed works. Scanned images of the actual pages, rather than transcriptions, recreate the works *as they first appeared.*

Now for the first time, these high-quality digital scans of original works are available via print-on-demand, making them readily accessible to libraries, students, independent scholars, and readers of all ages.

For our initial release we have created seven robust collections to form one the world's most comprehensive catalogs of 18th century works.

Initial Gale ECCO Print Editions collections include:

History and Geography
Rich in titles on English life and social history, this collection spans the world as it was known to eighteenth-century historians and explorers. Titles include a wealth of travel accounts and diaries, histories of nations from throughout the world, and maps and charts of a world that was still being discovered. Students of the War of American Independence will find fascinating accounts from the British side of conflict.

Social Science

Delve into what it was like to live during the eighteenth century by reading the first-hand accounts of everyday people, including city dwellers and farmers, businessmen and bankers, artisans and merchants, artists and their patrons, politicians and their constituents. Original texts make the American, French, and Industrial revolutions vividly contemporary.

Medicine, Science and Technology

Medical theory and practice of the 1700s developed rapidly, as is evidenced by the extensive collection, which includes descriptions of diseases, their conditions, and treatments. Books on science and technology, agriculture, military technology, natural philosophy, even cookbooks, are all contained here.

Literature and Language

Western literary study flows out of eighteenth-century works by Alexander Pope, Daniel Defoe, Henry Fielding, Frances Burney, Denis Diderot, Johann Gottfried Herder, Johann Wolfgang von Goethe, and others. Experience the birth of the modern novel, or compare the development of language using dictionaries and grammar discourses.

Religion and Philosophy

The Age of Enlightenment profoundly enriched religious and philosophical understanding and continues to influence present-day thinking. Works collected here include masterpieces by David Hume, Immanuel Kant, and Jean-Jacques Rousseau, as well as religious sermons and moral debates on the issues of the day, such as the slave trade. The Age of Reason saw conflict between Protestantism and Catholicism transformed into one between faith and logic -- a debate that continues in the twenty-first century.

Law and Reference

This collection reveals the history of English common law and Empire law in a vastly changing world of British expansion. Dominating the legal field is the *Commentaries of the Law of England* by Sir William Blackstone, which first appeared in 1765. Reference works such as almanacs and catalogues continue to educate us by revealing the day-to-day workings of society.

Fine Arts

The eighteenth-century fascination with Greek and Roman antiquity followed the systematic excavation of the ruins at Pompeii and Herculaneum in southern Italy; and after 1750 a neoclassical style dominated all artistic fields. The titles here trace developments in mostly English-language works on painting, sculpture, architecture, music, theater, and other disciplines. Instructional works on musical instruments, catalogs of art objects, comic operas, and more are also included.

The BiblioLife Network

This project was made possible in part by the BiblioLife Network (BLN), a project aimed at addressing some of the huge challenges facing book preservationists around the world. The BLN includes libraries, library networks, archives, subject matter experts, online communities and library service providers. We believe every book ever published should be available as a high-quality print reproduction; printed on-demand anywhere in the world. This insures the ongoing accessibility of the content and helps generate sustainable revenue for the libraries and organizations that work to preserve these important materials.

The following book is in the "public domain" and represents an authentic reproduction of the text as printed by the original publisher. While we have attempted to accurately maintain the integrity of the original work, there are sometimes problems with the original work or the micro-film from which the books were digitized. This can result in minor errors in reproduction. Possible imperfections include missing and blurred pages, poor pictures, markings and other reproduction issues beyond our control. Because this work is culturally important, we have made it available as part of our commitment to protecting, preserving, and promoting the world's literature.

GUIDE TO FOLD-OUTS MAPS and OVERSIZED IMAGES

The book you are reading was digitized from microfilm captured over the past thirty to forty years. Years after the creation of the original microfilm, the book was converted to digital files and made available in an online database.

In an online database, page images do not need to conform to the size restrictions found in a printed book. When converting these images back into a printed bound book, the page sizes are standardized in ways that maintain the detail of the original. For large images, such as fold-out maps, the original page image is split into two or more pages

Guidelines used to determine how to split the page image follows:

• Some images are split vertically; large images require vertical and horizontal splits.
• For horizontal splits, the content is split left to right.
• For vertical splits, the content is split from top to bottom.
• For both vertical and horizontal splits, the image is processed from top left to bottom right.

AN
APOLOGY
FOR
CHRISTIANITY.

AN

APOLOGY

FOR

CHRISTIANITY,

IN

A SERIES of LETTERS,

ADDRESSED TO

EDWARD GIBBON, Esq.

Author of the History of the Decline and Fall of the Roman Empire.

BY

R. WATSON, D.D F.R.S.

AND REGIUS PROFESSOR OF DIVINITY IN THE UNIVERSITY OF CAMBRIDGE.

FIFTH EDITION

LONDON

Printed for T Evans in the Strand, and in the Great Market, Bury St Edmund's, J and J Merrill, Cambridge, J Fletcher, and Prince and Cooke, Oxford, P Hill, Edinburgh, and W M'Kenzie, Dublin

M DCC XCI

I KNOW not whether I may be allowed, without the imputation of vanity, to exprefs the fatisfaction I felt on being told by my Bookfeller, that another Edition of the *Apology for Chriftianity* was wanted. It is a fatisfaction, however, in which vanity has no part; it is altogether founded in the delightful hope, that I may have been, in a fmall degree, inftrumental in recommending the Religion of Chrift to the attention of fome, who might not otherwife have confidered it, with

b   that

that ferious and unprejudiced difpofition which its impoitance requires.

The celebrity of the woik
which gave rife to this Apology,
has, no doubt, principally contii-
buted to its circulation : could I
have enteitained a thought, that
it would have been called for fo
many years after its firft publication, I would have endeavoured
to have rendeied it more intrin-
fecally worthy the public regard.
It becomes not me however to
depieciate what the world has
approved ; iather let me exprefs
an earneft wifh, that thofe who
diflike not this little Book, will

I peiufe

peruse larger ones on the same subject · in them they will see the defects of this so abundantly supplied, as will, I trust, convince them, that the Christian Religion is not a system of superstition, invented by enthusiasts, and patronized by statesmen, for secular ends, but a revelation of the will of God.

London,
March 10, 1791.

LETTER FIRST.

SIR,

IT would give me much uneasi-ness to be reputed an enemy to free inquiry in religious matters, or as capable of being animated into any degree of perfonal malevolence againft thofe who differ from me in opinion. On the contrary, I look upon the right of private judgment, in every concern refpecting God and ourfelves, as fuperior to the controul of human authority; and have ever regarded free difquifition as the beft mean of illuftrating the doctrine, and

B   eftablifh-

eftablifhing the truth of Chriftianity. Let the followers of Mahomet, and the zealots of the church of Rome, fupport their feveral religious fyftems by damping every effort of the human intellect to pry into the foundations of their faith . but never can it become a Chriftian, to be afraid of being afked a *reafon of the faith that is in him*; nor a Proteftant, to be ftudious of enveloping his religion in myftery and ignorance ; nor the church of England, to abandon that moderation by which fhe permits every individual *et fentire quæ velit, et quæ fentiat dicere.*

It is not, Sir, without fome reluctance, that, under the influence of thefe opinions, I have prevailed upon myfelf to addrefs thefe letters to you; and

and you will attribute to the fame
motive my not having given you
this trouble fooner. I had moreover
an expectation, that the tafk would
have been undertaken by fome perfon capable of doing greater juftice
to the fubject, and more worthy of
your attention. Perceiving, however,
that the two laft chapters, the fifteenth
in particular, of your very laborious
and claffical hiftory of the Decline
and Fall of the Roman Empire, had
made upon many an impreffion not
at all advantageous to Chriftianity;
and that the filence of others, of the
Clergy efpecially, began to be looked
upon as an acquiefcence in what
you had therein advanced; I have
thought it my duty, with the utmoft
refpect and good-will towards you,

B 2   to

to take the liberty of fuggefting to
your confideration a few remarks
upon fome of the paffages which
have been efteemed (whether you
meant that they fhould be fo efteemed or not) as powerfully militating
againft that revelation, which ftill is
to many, what it formerly was *to the
Greeks—foolifhnefs*; but which we
deem to be true, to *be the power of
God unto falvation to every one that
believeth.*

To the inquiry by what means the
Chriftian faith obtained fo remarkable a victory over the eftablifhed religions of the earth, you rightly anfwer, By the evidence of the doctrine itfelf, and the ruling providence
of its Author. But afterwards, in af-
figning

figning for this aftonifhing event five fecondary caufes, derived from the paffions of the human heart and the general circumftances of mankind, you feem to fome to have infinuated, that Chriftianity, like other impof- tures, might have made its way in the world, though its origin had been as human as the means by which you fuppofe it was fpread. It is no wifh or intention of mine, to faften the odium of this infinuation upon you : I fhall fimply endeavour to fhew, that the caufes you produce are either inadequate to the attainment of the end propofed; or that their efficien- cy, great as you imagine it, was de- rived from other principles than thofe you have thought proper to mention.

Your

FIRST CAUSE

Your first cause is, "the inflexible, and, if you may use the expression, the intolerant zeal of the Christians, derived, it is true, from the Jewish religion, but purified from the narrow and unsocial spirit which, instead of inviting, had detened the Gentiles from embracing the law of Moses."— Yes, Sir, we are agreed that the zeal of the Christians was inflexible ; *neither death, nor life, nor principalities, nor powers, nor things present, nor things to come,* could bend it into a separation *from the love of God, which was in Christ Jesus then Lord.* It was an inflexible obstinacy, in not blaspheming the name of Christ, which every where exposed them to persecution ; and which even your amiable and philosophic Pliny thought
proper,

yes
inflexible
+
intolerant.

propei, for want of othei ciimes, to punish with death in the Christians of his province.—We aie agieed, too, that the zeal of the Christians was intolerant; foi it denounced *tribulation and anguish upon every soul of man that did evil, of the Jew first, and also of the Gentile:* it would not toleiate in Christian woiship thofe who fupplicated the image of Cæfai, who bowed down at the altais of Paganifm, who mixed with the votaries of Venus, or wallowed in the filth of Bacchanalian feftivals.

But though we are thus far agreed with refpect to the inflexibility and intolerance of Christian zeal, yet, as to the principle from which it was derived, we are *toto cælo* divided in opinion. You deduce it from the Jewish

B 4   reli-

religion ; I would refer it to a more adequate and a more obvious source, a full persuasion of the truth of Christianity. What ! think you that it was a zeal derived from the unsocial spirit of Judaism, which inspired Peter with courage to upbraid the whole people of the Jews in the very capital of Judea, with having *delivered up Jesus, with having denied him in the presence of Pilate, with having desired a murderer to be granted them in his stead, with having killed the Prince of life?* Was it from this principle that the same apostle, in conjunction with John, when summoned, not before the dregs of the people (whose judgments they might have been supposed capable of misleading, and whose resentment they might have despised), but before the rulers and

the

the elders and the scribes, the dread tribunal of the Jewish nation, and commanded by them to teach no more in the name of Jesus—boldly answered, *that they could not but speak the things which they had seen and heard?* *They had seen with their eyes, they had handled with their hands, the word of life* , and no human jurisdiction could deter them from being faithful witnesses of what they had seen and heard. Here then you may perceive the genuine and undoubted origin of that zeal, which you ascribe to what appears to me a very insufficient cause, and which the Jewish rulers were so far from considering as the ordinary effect of their religion, that they were exceedingly at a loss how to account for it: —*now when they saw the boldness of Pe-*

ter

ter and John, and perceived that they were unlearned and ignorant men, they marvelled. The Apostles, heedless of consequences, and regardless of every thing but truth, openly every where professed themselves witnesses of the resurrection of Christ ; and with a confidence which could proceed from nothing but conviction, and which pricked the Jews to the heart, bade *the house of Israel know assuredly, that God had made that same Jesus, whom they had crucified, both Lord and Christ.*

I mean not to produce these instances of apostolic zeal as direct proofs of the truth of Christianity ; for every religion, nay, every absurd sect of every religion, has had its zealots, who have not scrupled to maintain their principles at the ex-
pence

pence of their lives, and we ought
no more to infer the truth of Christianity from the mere zeal of its pro-
pagators, than the truth of Maho-
metanism from that of a Turk.
When a man suffers himself to be
covered with infamy, pillaged of his
property, and dragged at last to the
block or the stake, rather than give
up his opinion, the proper inference
is, not that his opinion is true, but
that he believes it to be true : and a
question of serious discussion immediately presents itself—upon what
foundation has he built his belief?
This is often an intricate inquiry, including in it a vast compass of human learning. a Bramin or a Man-
darin, who should observe a mis-
sionary attesting the truth of Christianity with his blood, would, not-

with-

withftanding, have a right to afk many queftions, before it could be expected that he fhould give an affent to our faith. In the cafe indeed of the Apoftles, the inquiry would be much lefs perplexed; fince it would briefly refolve itfelf into this—whether they were credible reporters of facts which they themfelves profeffed to have feen :—and it would be an eafy matter to fhew, that their zeal in attefting what they were certainly competent to judge of, could not proceed from any alluring profpect of worldly intereft or ambition, or from any other probable motive than a love of truth.

But the credibility of the Apoftles' teftimony, or their competency to judge of the facts which they relate, is

is not now to be examined; the queftion before us fimply relates to the
principle by which their zeal was
excited: and it is a matter of real
aftonifhment to me, that any one
converfant with the hiftory of the
firft propagation of Chriftianity, acquainted with the oppofition it every
where met with from the people of
the Jews, and aware of the repug-
nancy which muft ever fubfift between its tenets and thofe of Ju-
daifm, fhould ever think of deriv-
ing the zeal of the primitive Chriftians from the Jewifh religion.

Both Jew and Chriftian, indeed,
believed in one God, and abomi-
nated idolatry; but this deteftation
of idolatry, had it been unaccompa-
nied with the belief of the refurrection

tion of Chrift, would probably have been juft as inefficacious in exciting the zeal of the Chriftian to undertake the converfion of the Gentile world, as it had for ages been in exciting that of the Jew. But fuppofing, what I think you have not proved, and what I am certain cannot be admitted without proof, that a zeal derived from the Jewifh religion infpired the firft Chriftians with fortitude to oppofe themfelves to the inftitutions of Paganifm; what was it that encouraged them to attempt the converfion of their own countrymen? Amongft the Jews they met with no fuperftitious obfervances of idolatrous rites; and therefore amongft them could have no opportunity of " declaring and confirming their zealous oppofition to Polytheifm, or

of

of fortifying by frequent proteſtations
their attachment to the Chriſtian
faith." Here then, at leaſt, the cauſe
you have aſſigned for Chriſtian zeal
ceaſes to operate, and we muſt look
out for ſome other principle than a
zeal againſt idolatry, or we ſhall never be able ſatisfactorily to explain
the ardour with which the Apoſtles
preſſed the diſciples of Moſes to become the diſciples of Chriſt.

Again, does a determined oppoſition to, and an open abhorrence of,
every the minuteſt part of an eſtabliſhed religion, appear to you to be
the moſt likely method of conciliat-
ing to another faith thoſe who profeſs
it ? The Chriſtians, you contend,
could neither mix with the Heathens
in their convivial entertainments, nor
partake with them in the celebration
of

of their folemn feftivals, they could
neither affociate with them in their hy-
meneal nor funereal rites; they could
not cultivate their arts, or be fpectators
of their fhows; in fhort, in order to
efcape the rites of Polytheifm, they
were in your opinion obliged to re-
nounce the commerce of mankind,
and all the offices and amufements
of life. Now, how fuch an extravagant and intemperate zeal as you
here defcribe, can, humanly fpeaking, be confidered as one of the chief
caufes of the quick propagation of
Chriftianity, in oppofition to all the
eftablifhed powers of Paganifm, is a
circumftance I can by no means
comprehend. The Jefuit miffionaries, whofe human prudence no one
will queftion, were quite of a contrary
way of thinking; and brought a deferved cenfure upon themfelves for
not

not fcrupling to propagate the faith of Chrift, by indulging to then Pagan converts a frequent ufe of idolatrous ceremonies. Upon the whole it appears to me, that the Chriftians were in no wife indebted to the Jewifh religion for the zeal with which they propagated the gofpel amongft Jews as well as Gentiles ; and that fuch a zeal as you defcribe, let its principle be what you pleafe, could never have been devifed by any human underftanding as a probable mean of promoting the progrefs of a reformation in religion, much lefs could it have been thought of or adopted by a few ignorant and unconnected men.

In expatiating upon this fubject you have taken an opportunity of remark-

remarking, that " the contemporaries of Moses and Joshua had beheld
with careless indifference the most
amazing miracles—and that, in contradiction to every known principle
of the human mind, that singular
people (the Jews) seems to have
yielded a stronger and more ready
assent to the traditions of their remote
anceftors than to the evidence of
their own senses." This observation
bears hard upon the veracity of the
Jewish scriptures; and, was it true,
would force us either to reject them,
or to admit a position as extraordinary
as a miracle itself—that the testimony of others produced in the human mind a stronger degree of conviction, concerning a matter of fact,
than the testimony of the senses themselves. It happens however, in the
present

present case, that we are under no
necessity of either rejecting the Jewish
scriptures, or of admitting such an
absurd position; for the fact is not
true, that the contemporaries of
Moses and Joshua beheld with careless indifference the miracles related
in the Bible to have been performed
in their favour.   That these miracles
were not sufficient to awe the Israel-
ites into an uniform obedience to the
Theocracy, cannot be denied; but
whatever reasons may be thought
best adapted to account for the pro-
pensity of the Jews to idolatry, and
their frequent defection from the
worship of the one true God, a "stubborn incredulity" cannot be admitted as one of them.

To men, indeed, whose understandings

ftandings have been enlightened by
the Chriftian revelation, and enlarged
by all the aids of human learning;
who are under no temptations to idolatry from without, and whofe reafon
from within would revolt at the idea
of worfhipping the infinite Author of
the univerfe under any created fym-
bol;—to men who are compelled,
by the utmoft exertion of their reafon,
to admit as an irrefragable truth,
what puzzles the firft principles of
all reafoning—the eternal exiftence
of an uncaufed Being;—and who are
confcious that they cannot give a
full account of any one phænomenon
in nature, from the rotation of the
great orbs of the univerfe to the ger-
mination of a blade of grafs, without
having recourfe to him as the primary
incomprehenfible caufe of it;—and
who,

who, from feeing him every where, have, by a ftrange fatality (convert- ing an excefs of evidence into a prin- ciple of difbelief), at times doubted concerning his exiftence any where, and made the very univerfe their God;—to men of fuch a ftamp, it appears almoft an incredible thing, that any human being which had feen the order of nature interrupted, or the uniformity of its courfe fuf- pended, though but for a moment, fhould ever afterwards lofe the im- preffion of reverential awe which they apprehend would have been ex- cited in their minds. But whatever effect the vifible interpofition of the Deity might have in removing the fcepticifm, or confirming the faith, of a few philofophers, it is with me a very great doubt, whether the people in general of our days would be more ftrongly affected by it than they appear to have been in the days of Mofes.

Was any people under heaven to efcape the certain deftruction impending over them, from the clofe purfuit of an enraged and irrefiftible enemy, by feeing the waters of the ocean *becoming a wall to them on their right hand and on their left*, they would, I apprehend, be agitated by the very fame paffions we are told the Ifraelites were, when they faw the fea, returning to his ftrength, and fwallowing up the hoft of Pharaoh; they *would fear the Lord, they would believe the Lord*, and they would exprefs their faith and their fear by praifing the Lord :—they would not be-

hold

hold such a great work with *careless indifference*, but with astonishment and terror; **nor** would you be able to detect the flighteft veftige of *ftubborn incredulity* in their fong of gratitude. No length of time would be able to blot from their minds the memory of fuch a tranfaction, or induce a doubt concerning its Author; though future hunger and thirft might make them call out for water and bread, with a defponding and rebellious importunity.

But it was not at the Red Sea only that the Ifraelites regarded with fomething more than a *careless indifference* the amazing miracles which God had wrought, for, when the law was declared to them from mount Sinai, *all the people faw the thunder-*

thunderings, and the lightnings, and the noise of the tempest, and the mountains smoking; and when the people saw it, they removed and stood afar off: and they said unto Moses, Speak thou with us, and we will hear; but let not God speak with us, lest we die.—This again, Sir, is the Scripture account of the language of the contemporaries of Mofes and Joshua; and I leave it to you to confider whether this is the language of *stubborn incredulity, and carelefs indifference.*

We are told in Scripture, too, that whilst any of the *contemporaries* of Mofes and Joshua were alive, the whole people ferved the Lord: the impreffion which a fight of the miracles had made, was never effaced—nor the obedience, which might have

been

been expected as a natural confe
quence, refufed—till Mofes and Jofhua, and all their contempoiaries,
were gathered unto their fathers ; till
another generation after then arofe,
which knew not the Lord, nor yet the
works which he had done for Ifrael —
But *the people ferved the Lord all the*
days of Jofhua, and all the days of the
elders that outlived Jofhua, who had feen
all the great works of the Lord that he
did for Ifrael.

I am far fiom thinking you, Sii,
unacquainted with Scripture, or defirous of finking the weight of its teftimony ; but as the words of the hif-
toiy fiom which you muft have de-
iived your obfeivation, will not fup-
poit you in imputing *careless indiffe-*
rence to the contempoiaries of Mofes,

or

or *stubborn incredulity* to the forefa-
thers of the Jews, I know not what
can have induced you to pass so se-
vere a censure upon them, except
that you look upon a lapse into idolatry as a proof of infidelity. In
answer to this I would remark, that
with equal foundness of argument we
ought to infer, that every one who
transgresses a religion, disbelieves it,
and that every individual, who in
any community incurs civil pains and
penalties, is a disbeliever of the exist-
ence of the authority by which they
are inflicted. The sanctions of the
Mosaic law were, in your opinion,
terminated within the narrow limits
of this life ; in that particular, then,
they must have resembled the sanctions of all other civil laws . *transgress
and die* is the language of every one

of them, as well as that of Mofes; and I know not what reafon we have to expect that the Jews, who were animated by the fame hopes of temporal rewards, impelled by the fame fears of temporal punifhments, with the reft of mankind, fhould have been fo fingular in their conduct, as never to have liftened to the clamours of paffion before the ftill voice of reafon , as never to have preferred a prefent gratification of fenfe, in the lewd celebration of idolatrous rites, before the rigid obfervance of irkfome ceremonies.

Before I releafe you from the trouble of this Letter, I cannot help obferving, that I could have wifhed you had furnifhed your reader with Limborch's anfwers to the objections of

C 2   the

the Jew Orobio, concerning the perpetual obligation of the law of Mofes. You have indeed mentioned Limborch with refpect, in a fhort note . but though you have ftudioufly put into the mouths of the Judaifing Chriftians in the apoftolic days, and with great ftrength inferted into your text, whatever has been faid by Orobio or others againft Chriftianity, from the fuppofed perpetuity of the Mofaic difpenfation; yet you have not favoured us with any one of the numerous replies which have been made to thefe feemingly ftrong objections. You are pleafed, it is true, to fay, "that the induftry of our learned divines has abundantly explained the ambiguous language of the Old Teftament, and the ambiguous conduct of the apof-

tolic

tolic teachers." It requires, Sir, no learned induſtry to explain what is ſo obvious and ſo expreſs, that he who runs may read it. The language of the Old Teſtament is this *Behold, the days come, ſaith the Lord, that I will make a new covenant with the houſe of Iſrael, and with the houſe of Judah, not according to the covenant that I made with their fathers, in the day that I took them by the hand to bring them out of the land of Egypt.* This, methinks, is a clear and ſolemn declaration—there is no ambiguity at all in it—that the covenant with Moſes was not to be perpetual, but was in ſome future time to give way to a *new covenant.* I will not detain you with an explanation of what Moſes himſelf has ſaid upon this ſubject; but you may try, if you pleaſe, whe-

ther

ther you can apply the following declaration, which Mofes made to the
Jews, to any prophet or fucceffion of
prophets, with the fame propriety
that you can to Jefus Chrift.—*The
Lord thy God will raife up unto thee a
Prophet from the midft of thee, of thy
brethren, like unto me: unto him fhall
ye hearken* If you think this ambiguous or obfcure, I anfwer, That it
is not a hiftory, but a prophecy; and,
as fuch, unavoidably liable to fome
degree of obfcurity, till interpreted
by the event.

Nor was the conduct of the
Apoftles more ambiguous than the
language of the Old Teftament. they
did not indeed at firft comprehend
the whole of the nature of the new
difpenfation; and when they did underftand

derſtand it better, they did not think proper upon every occaſion to uſe their Chriſtian liberty, but, with true Chriſtian charity, accommodated themſelves in matters of indifference to the prejudices of their weaker brethren. But he who changes his conduct with a change of ſentiments, proceeding from an increaſe of knowledge, is not ambiguous in his conduct ; nor ſhould he be accuſed of a culpable duplicity, who in a matter of the laſt importance endeavours to conciliate the good-will of all, by conforming in a few innocent obſervances to the particular perſuaſions of different men.

One remark more, and I have done. In your account of the Gnoſtics, you have given us a very minute catalogue of the objections

which

which they made to the authority of Mofes, from his account of
the creation, of the patriarchs, of
the law, and of the attributes
of the Deity. I have not leifure
to examine whether the Gnoftics
of former ages really made all the
objections you have mentioned, I
take it for granted, upon your authority, that they did. but I am certain, if they did, that the Gnoftics of
modern times have no reafon to be
puffed up with their knowledge, or
to be had in admiration as men of
fubtile penetration or refined erudition: they are all miferable copiers
of their brethren of antiquity ; and
neither Morgan, nor Tindal, nor
Bolingbroke, nor Voltaire, have been
able to produce fcarce a fingle new
objection. You think that the Fathers have not properly anfwered the
Gnoftics.

Gnoſtics. I make no queſtion, Sir, you are able to anſwer them to your own ſatisfaction, and informed of every thing that has been ſaid by our *induſtrious divines* upon the ſubject, and we ſhould have been glad, if it had fallen in with your plan to have adminiſtered together with the poiſon its antidote. but ſince that is not the caſe, left its malignity ſhould ſpread too far, I muſt juſt mention it to my younger readers, that Leland and others, in their replies to the modern Deiſts, have given very full, and, as many learned men apprehend, very ſatisfactory anſwers to every one of the objections which you have derived from the Gnoſtic hereſy.

I am, &c.

C 5 LET-

LETTER SECOND.

SIR,

"THE doctrine of a future life, improved by every additional circumstance which could give weight and efficacy to that important truth," is the second of the causes to which you attribute the quick increase of Christianity. Now if we impartially consider the circumstances of the persons to whom the doctrine, not simply of a future life, but of a future life accompanied with punishments as well as rewards; not only of the immortality of the soul,

foul, but of the immortality of the
foul accompanied with that of the
refurrection, was delivered; I cannot be of opinion that, abftracted
from the fupernatural teftimony by
which it was enforced, it could have
met with any very extenfive reception amongft them.

It was not that kind of future life
which they expected; it did not
hold out to them the punifhments
of the infernal regions as *aniles fa-
bulas* To the queftion, *Quid fi poft
mortem maneant animi?* they could
not anfwer with Cicero and the philofophers—*Beatos effe concedo*; becaufe there was a great probability
that it might be quite otherwife
with them. I am not to learn that
there are paffages to be picked up

in

in the writings of the antients which
might be produced as proofs of their
expecting a future state of punishment for the flagitious, but this opinion was worn out of credit before
the time of our Saviour: the whole
disputation in the first book of the
Tusculan Questions, goes upon the
other supposition. Nor was the absurdity of the doctrine of future punishments confined to the writings of the
philosophers, or the circles of the
learned and polite; for Cicero, to mention no others, makes no secret of
it in his public pleadings before the
people at large. You yourself, Sir,
have referred to his oration for Clu-
entius: in this oration, you may remember, he makes great mention of
a very abandoned fellow, who had
forged I know not how many wills,
murdered

murdered I know not how many
wives, and perpetrated a thoufand
other villanies ; yet even to this profligate, by name Oppianicus, he is
perfuaded that death was not the occafion of any evil *. Hence, I think,
we may conclude, that fuch of the
Romans as were not wholly infect-
ed with the annihilating notions of
Epicurus, but entertained (whether
from remote tradition or enlightened
argumentation) hopes of a future
life, had no manner of expectation
of fuch a life as included in it the
feverity of punifhment denounced in

* Nam nunc quidem quid tandem mali illi
mors attulit ? nifi forte ineptiis ac fabulis duci-
mur, ut exiftimemus apud inferos impiorum fup-
plicia perferre, ac plures illic offendiffe inimi-
cos quam hic reliquiffe—quæ fi falfa fint, id
quod omnes intelligunt, &c.

the

the Chriſtian ſcheme againſt the wicked.

Nor was it that kind of future life which they wiſhed : they would have been glad enough of an Elyſium which could have admitted into it men who had ſpent this life in the perpetration of every vice which can debaſe and pollute the human heart. To abandon every ſeducing gratification of ſenſe, to pluck up every latent root of ambition, to ſubdue every impulſe of revenge, to diveſt themſelves of every inveterate habit in which their glory and their pleaſure conſiſted ; to do all this and more, before they could look up to the doctrine of a future life without terror and amazement, was not, one would think, an eaſy undertaking.

nor

nor was it likely that many would
forsake the religious institutions of
their anceftors, fet at nought the
gods under whofe aufpices the Ca-
pitol had been founded, and Rome
made miftrefs of the world; and fuffer themfelves to be perfuaded into
the belief of a tenet, the very mention of which made Fel x tremble,
by any thing lefs than a full conviction of the fupernatural authority of
thofe who taught it.

The feveral fchools of Gentile
philofophy had difcuffed, with no
fmall fubtlety, every argument which
reafon could fuggeft, for and againft
the immortality of the foul, and
thofe uncertain glimmerings of the
light of nature would have prepared
the minds of the learned for the re-

ception of the full illuſtration of this ſubject by the goſpel, had not the reſurrection been a part of the doctrine therein advanced. But that this corporal frame, which is hourly mouldering away, and reſolved at laſt into the undiſtinguiſhed maſs of elements from which it was at firſt derived, ſhould ever be *clothed with immortality, that this corruptible ſhould ever put on incorruption*, is a truth ſo far removed from the apprehenſion of philoſophical reſearch, ſo diſſonant from the common conceptions of mankind, that amongſt all ranks and perſuaſions of men it was eſteemed an impoſſible thing. At Athens the philoſophers had liſtened with patience to St. Paul, whilſt they conceived him but a *ſetter forth of ſtrange gods*, but as ſoon as they comprehended

prehended that by the ἀνάςασις he meant the refurrection, they turned from him with contempt. It was principally the infifting upon the fame topic, which made Feflus think *that much learning had made him mad.* And the queftions, *How are the dead raifed up?* and, *With what body do they come?* feem, by Paul's folicitude to anfwer them with fulnefs and precifion, to have been not unfrequently propofed to him by thofe who were defirous of becoming Chriftians.

The doctrine of a future life then, as promulged in the gofpel, being neither agreeable to the expectations, nor correfponding with the wifhes, nor conformable to the reafon, of the Gentiles, I can difcover no motive (fetting afide the true one, the divine

power

power of its firft preachers) which could induce them to receive it; and, in confequence of their belief, to conform their loofe morals to the rigid ftandard of gofpel purity, upon the mere authority of a few contemptible fifhermen of Judea. And even you yourfelf, Sir, feem to have changed your opinion concerning the efficacy of the expectation of a future life in converting the Heathens, when you obferve, in the following chapter, that "the Pagan multitude referving their gratitude for temporal benefits alone, rejected the ineftimable prefent of life and immortality which was offered to mankind by Jefus of Nazareth."

Montefquieu is of opinion that it will ever be impoffible for Chriftianit tianity to establish itself in China and the east, from this circumstance, that it prohibits a plurality of wives. How then could it have been possible for it to have pervaded the voluptuous capital, and traversed the utmost limits, of the empire of Rome, by the feeble efforts of human industry, or human knavery?

But the Gentiles, you are of opinion, were converted by their fears; and reckon the doctrines of Christ's speedy appearance, of the millennium, and of the general conflagration, amongst those additional circumstances which gave weight to that concerning a future state. Before I proceed to the examination of the efficiency of these several circumstances in alarming the apprehensions fions of the Gentiles, what if I fhould grant your pofition ? ftill the main queftion recurs—From what fource did they derive the fears which converted them ? Not furely from the mere human labours of men, who were every where fpoken againft, made a fpectacle of, and confidered as the filth of the world, and the off-fcouring of all things—not furely from the human powers of him who profeffed himfelf *rude in fpeech, in bodily prefence contemptibe*, and a defpifer of *the excellency of fpeech, and the enticing words of man's wifdom.* No, fuch wretched inftruments were but ill fitted to infpire the haughty and the learned Romans with any other paffions than thofe of pity or contempt.

Now,

Now, Sir, if you pleafe, we will confider that univerfal expectation of the approaching end of the world, which, you think, had fuch great influence in converting the Pagans to the profeffion of Chriftianity. The near approach, you fay, of this wonderful event had been predicted by the Apoftles, " though the revolution of feventeen centuries has inftructed us not to prefs too clofely the myfterious language of prophecy and revelation." That this opinion, even in the times of the Apoftles, had made its way into the Chriftian church, I readily admit, but that the Apoftles ever either predicted this event to others, or cherifhed the expectation of it in themfelves, does not feem probable to me. As this is a point of fome difficulty and im-

poitance,

poitance, you will fuffei me to explain it at fome length.

It muft be owned that there aie
feveial paffages in the wiitings of the
Apoftles, which, at the firft view,
feem to countenance the opinion you
have adopted Now, fays St. Paul, in
his Epiftle to the Romans, *it is high
time to awake out of fleep, for now is our
falvation neorei than when we believed.
The night is far fpent, the day is at
hand.* And in his Fuft Epiftle to the
Theffalonians he comfoits fuch of
them as weie fouowing for the lofs
of their friends, by affuiing them
that they were not loft for evei; but
that the Loid, when he came, would
biing them with him; and that they
would not, in the paiticipation of
any bleffings, be in any wife behind
thofe

those who should happen then to be alive · *we*, says he (the Christians of whatever age or country, agreeable to a frequent use of the pronoun *we*), *which are alive, and remain unto the coming of the Lord, shall not prevent them which are asleep; for the Lord himself shall descend from heaven with a shout, with the voice of the archangel, and with the trump of God, and the dead in Christ shall rise first; then we which are alive, and remain, shall be caught up together with them in the clouds, to meet the Lord.* In his Epistle to the Philippians he exhorts his Christian brethren not to disquiet themselves with carking cares about their temporal concerns, from this powerful consideration, that the Lord was at hand. *Let your moderation be known unto all men; the*

Lord

*Lord is at hand , be careful about no-
thing.* The apoftle to the Hebrews
inculcates the fame doctrine, admo-
nifhing his converts *to provoke one
another to love, and to good works , and
fo much the more, as they faw the day
approaching.* The age in which the
Apoftles lived, is frequently called
by them the end of the world, the
laft days, the laft hour. I think it
unneceffary, Sir, to trouble you with
an explication of thefe and other
fimilar texts of fcripture, which are
ufually adduced in fupport of your
opinion ; fince I hope to be able to
give you a direct proof, that the
Apoftles neither comforted themfelves, nor encouraged others, with
the delightful hope of feeing their
mafter coming again into the world.
It is evident then that St. John, who

fur-

survived all the other Apostles, could
not have had any such expectation;
since in the Book of the Revelation,
the future events of the Christian
church, which were not to take place,
many of them, till a long series of
years after his death, and some of
which have not yet been accomplished, are there minutely described.
St. Peter, in like manner, strongly
intimates, that the day of the Lord
might be said to be at hand, though
it was at the distance of a thousand
years or more; for in replying to
the taunt of those who did then, or
should in future ask, *Where is the
promise of his coming?* he says, *Beloved, be not ignorant of this one thing,
that one day is with the Lord as a thousand years, and a thousand years as one
day. The Lord is not slack concerning*

his

his promife, as fome men count flackneſ.
And he fpeaks of putting off his
tabernacle, as the Lord had fhewed
him, and of his endeavour, that the
Chriftians after his deceafe might be
able to have thefe things in remem-
brance: So that it is paft a doubt,
he could not be of opinion, that the
Lord would come in his time.   As
to St. Paul, upon a partial view of
whofe writings the doctrine concerning the fpeedy coming of Chrift is
principally founded; it is manifeft,
that he was confcious he fhould not
live to fee it, notwithftanding the
expreffion before mentioned, *we
which are alive*, for he foretels his
own death in exprefs terms—*the
time of my departure is at hand*, and
he fpeaks of his reward, not as immediately to be conferred on him;
but

but as laid up, and reserved for him till some future day—*I have fought a good fight, I have finished my course; henceforth there is laid up for me a crown of righteousness, which the Lord, the righteous judge, shall give me at that day.* There is moreover one passage in his writings, which is so express, and full to the purpose, that it will put the matter I think beyond all doubt; it occurs in his second Epistle to the Thessalonians : They, it seems, had either by misinterpreting some parts of his former letter to them, or by the preaching of some, who had not the spirit of truth, by some means or other, they had been led to expect the speedy coming of Christ, and been greatly disturbed in mind upon that account. To remove this error, he writes to them in the

D 2 follow-

following very folemn and affec-
tionate manner : *We befeech you, bre-*
thren, by the coming of our Lord Jefus
Chrift, and by our gathering together unto
him, that ye be not foon fhaken in mind,
or be troubled, neither by fpirit, nor by
word, nor by letter as from us, as that
the day of the Lord is at hand; let no
man deceive you by any means. He
then goes on to defcribe a falling
away, a great corruption of the Chriftian church, which was to happen
before the day of the Lord. Now
by this revelation of the man of fin,
this myftery of iniquity, which is to
be confumed with the fpirit of his
mouth, deftroyed by the brightnefs
of his coming, we have every reafon
to believe, is to be underftood the
paft and prefent abominations of the
church of Rome. How then can it
be

be said of Paul, who clearly forefaw this corruption above seventeen hundred years ago, that he expected the coming of the Lord in his own day? Let us press, Sir, the mysterio s language of prophecy and revelation, as closely as you please; but let us press it truly, and we may, perhaps, find reason from thence to receive, with less reluctance, a religion, which describes a corruption, the strangeness of which, had it not been foretold in unequivocal terms, might have amazed even a friend to Christianity.

I will produce you, Sir, a prophecy, which, the more closely you press it, the more reason you will have to believe, that the speedy coming of Christ could never have been *pre-*

D 3

dicted

dicted by the Apostles. Take it, as
translated by Bishop Newton : *But
the Spirit speaketh expressly, that in the
latter times, some shall apostatize from
the faith ; giving heed to erroneous spirits, and doctrines concerning demons,
through the hypocrisy of liars , having
their conscience seared with a red-hot
iron ; forbidding to marry, and commanding to abstain from meats.*—Here
you have an express prophecy—the
Spirit hath spoken it—that in the
latter times—not immediately, but
at some distant period—some should
apostatize from the faith—some, who
had been Christians, should in truth
be so no longer—but should give
heed to erroneous spirits, and doctrines concerning demons —Press
this expression closely, and you may,
perhaps, discover in it the erroneous
tenets,

tenets, and the demon of faint worship, of the church of Rome ;—
through the hypocrify of liars :—You
recognize, no doubt, the priefthood,
and the martyrologifts ,———having
their confcience feared with a red-
hot iron .—Callous, indeed, muft his
confcience be, who traffics in indul-
gences,—forbidding to marry, and
commanding to abftain from meats :
—This language needs no preffing ;
it difcovers, at once, the unhappy
votaries of monaftic life, and the
mortal fin of eating flefh on faft
days.

If, notwithftanding what has been
faid, you fhould ftill be of opinion,
that the Apoftles expected Chrift
would come in their time ; it will not
follow, that this their error ought in

any

any wife to diminish their authority
as preachers of the gospel. I am
sensible this position may alarm even
some well-wishers to Christianity;
and supply its enemies with what
they will think an irrefragable argument . The Apostles, they will say,
were inspired with the spirit of truth;
and yet they fell into a gross mistake,
concerning a matter of great importance : how is this to be reconciled?
Perhaps, in the following manner :
When the time of our Saviour's mi-
nistry was nearly at an end, he
thought proper to raise the spirits of
his disciples, who were quite cast
down with what he had told them
about his design of leaving them;
by promising, that he would send to
them the Holy Ghost, the Comforter,
the Spirit of truth; who should teach
them

them all things, and lead them into all truth. And we know, that this his promife was accomplifhed on the day of Pentecoft, when they were all filled with the Holy Ghoft; and we know farther, that from that time forward, they were enabled to fpeak with tongues, to work miracles, to preach the word with power, and to comprehend the myftery of the new difpenfation which was committed unto them. But we have no reafon from hence to conclude, that they were immediately infpired with the apprehenfion of whatever might be known; that they became acquainted with all kinds of truth: They were undoubtedly led into fuch truths as it was neceffary for them to know, in order to their converting the world to Chriftianity, but in

D 5

other

other things, they were probably left
to the exercise of their underftandings, as other men ufually are. But
furely they might be proper witneffes
of the life and refurrection of Chrift,
though they were not acquainted
with every thing which might have
been known, though, in particular,
they were ignorant of the precife
time when our Lord would come to
judge the world. It can be no im-
peachment, either of their integrity
as men, or their ability as hiftorians,
or their honefty as preachers of the
gofpel, that they were unacquainted
with what had never been revealed
to them, that they followed their
own underftandings where they had
no better light to guide them;
fpeaking from conjecture, when they
could not fpeak from certainty; of
them-

themfelves, when they had no commandment of the Lord. They knew but in part, and they prophefied but in part; and concerning this particular point, Jefus himfelf had told them, juft as he was about finally to leave them, that it was not for them to *know the times and the feafons, which the Father had put in his own power.* Nor is it to be wondered at, that the Apoftles were left in a ftate of uncertainty concerning the time in which Chrift fhould appear; fince beings far more exalted, and more highly favoured of heaven than they, were under an equal degree of ignorance: *Of that day,* fays our Saviour, *and of that hour, knoweth no one; no, not the angels which are in heaven, neither the Son, but the Father only.*——I am afraid, Sir, I have tired you with fcripture

D 6   quota-

quotations ; but if I have been fortunate enough to convince you, either
that the fpeedy coming of Chrift was
never expected, much lefs *predicted,*
by the Apoftles, or that their miftake in that particular expectation,
can in no degree diminifh the general
weight of their teftimony as hiftorians, I fhall not be forry for the *ennui*
I may have occafioned you.

The doctrine of the Millennium is
the fecond of the circumftances which
you produce, as giving weight to that
of a future ftate, and you reprefent
this doctrine as having been " care-
fully inculcated by a fucceffion of the
fathers, from Juftin Martyr and Ire-
næus down to Lactantius," and obferve that, when " the edifice of the
church was almoft completed, the
tempo-

temporary fupport was laid afide :"
and in the notes you refer us, as a
proof of what you advance, to " Irc-
næus, the difciple of Papias, who
had feen the apoftle St. John," and
to the fecond Dialogue of Juftin with
Tiypho.

I wifh, Sir, you had turned to Eu-
febius, for the character of this Papias, who had feen the apoftle St.
John, you would there have found
him reprefented as little better than a
credulous old woman, very averfe
from reading, but mightily given to
picking up ftories and traditions next
to fabulous, amongft which Eufe-
bius reckons this of the Millennium
one. Nor is it, I apprehend, quite
certain, that Papias ever faw, much
lefs difcourfed, as feems to be infinuated,

nuated, with the apoſtle St. John.
Euſebius thinks rather, that it was
John the preſbyter he had ſeen. But
what if he had ſeen the apoſtle himſelf? Many a weak-headed man had
undoubtedly ſeen him as well as Papias; and it would be hard indeed
upon Chriſtians, if they were compelled to receive as apoſtolical traditions the wild reveries of ancient en-
thuſiaſm, or ſuch crude conceptions
of ignorant fanaticiſm, as nothing
but the ruſt of antiquity can render
venerable.

As to the works of Juſtin, the very
dialogue you refer to contains a
proof, that the doctrine of the Millennium had not, even in his time, the
univerſal reception you have ſuppoſed; but that many Chriſtians of
pure

pure and pious principles rejected it. I wonder how this paſſage eſcaped you; but it may be that you followed Tillotſon, who himſelf followed Mede, and read in the original ȣ inſtead of αυ; and thus unwarily violated the idiom of the language, the ſenſe of the context, and the authority of the beſt editions *. In the note

---

* Juſtin, in anſwering the queſtion propoſed by Trypho, Whether the Chriſtians believed the doctrine of the Millennium, ſays, Ωμολογητα ȣ σοι και προτεϛο , οτι εγω μεν και αλλοι πολλοι ταυτα φρονȣμεν, ως και παντα επιϛασθε, τȣτι γενησομεϝο. Πολλȣ δ'ευ γϝι των της ΚΑΘΑΡΑΣ ΚΑΙ ΕΥΣΕΒΟΥΣ οντων Χριϛιϝων ΓΝΩΜΗΣ τȣτο μη γνωριξει, εσημα α σοι The note ſubjoined to this paſſage out of Juſtin, in Thalby's Ed an. 172⸳ is, [Π⸳ ȣȣδ'αυ και των ττς ραθαρα⸳] Medus (quem ſequitur Tillotſenus, Reg. Fidei per

note you obferve, that it is unnecefla-
ry for you to mention all the interme-
diate fathers between Juftin and Lactantius, as the fact, you fay, is not
difputed. In a man who has read
fo many books, and to fo good a
purpofe, he muft be captious indeed,
who cannot excufe fmall miftakes.
That unprejudiced regard to truth,
however, which is the great characteriftic of every diftinguifhed hifto-
rian, will, I am perfuaded, make you
thank me for recalling to your memory, that Origen, the moft learned

per iii. fect. 9, p 756, & feq.) legit των ε της
καθαρας. Vehementer errant viri præclari.

And in Jebb's Edit. an. 1719, we have the
following note Doctrinaitque de Millennio,
neque erat univerfalis ecclefiæ traditio, nec
opinio de fide recepta, &c.

o

of all the fathers, and Dionyſius, bi-
ſhop of Alexandria, uſually for his
immenſe erudition ſurnamed the
Great, were both of them prior to
Lactantius, and both of them im-
pugners of the Millennium doctrine.
Look, Sir, into Moſheim, or almoſt
any writer of eccleſiaſtical hiſtory, and
you will find the oppoſition of Origen and Dionyſius to this ſyſtem particularly noticed : look into ſo common an author as Whitby, and in
his learned treatiſe upon this ſubject,
you will find he has well proved
theſe two propoſitions · firſt, that
this opinion of the Millennium was
never generally received in the
church of Chriſt ; ſecondly, that
there is no juſt ground to think it
was derived from the Apoſtles. From
hence, I think, we may conclude,

that

that this Millennium doctrine (which, by the bye, though it be new modelled, is not yet thrown afide) could not have been any very ferviceable fcaffold in the erection of that mighty edifice, which has crufhed by the weight of its materials, and debafed by the elegance of its ftructure, the ftatelieft temples of heathen fuperftition. With thefe remarks, I take leave of the Millennium; juft obferving, that your third circumftance, the general conflagration, feems to be effectually included in your firft, the fpeedy coming of Chrift.

I am, &c.

LETTER THIRD.

SIR,

YOU esteem "the miraculous powers ascribed to the primitive church," as the third of the secondary causes of the rapid growth of Christianity. I should be willing to account the miracles, not merely ascribed to the primitive church, but really performed by the Apostles, as the one great primary cause of the conversion of the Gentiles. But waving this consideration, let us see whether the miraculous powers, which you ascribe to the primitive church,

were

were in any eminent degree calcu-
lated to spread the belief of Chriftianity amongft a great and an enlightened people.

They confifted, you tell us, " of
divine infpirations, conveyed fometimes in the form of a fleeping, fometimes of a waking vifion; and were
liberally beftowed on all ranks of
the faithful, on women as on elders,
on boys as well as upon bifhops."
" The defign of thefe vifions,"
you fay, " was for the moft part either to difclofe the future hiftory, or
to guide the prefent adminiftration
of the church." You fpeak of " the
expulfion of demons as an ordinary triumph of religion, ufually performed in a public manner; and
when the patient was relieved by the
fkill

skill or the power of the exorcist, the vanquished demon was heard to confefs, that he was one of the fabled gods of antiquity who had impioufly ufurped the adoration of mankind," and you reprefent even the miracle of the refurrection of the dead, as frequently performed on neceffary occafions.—Caft your eye, Sir, upon the church of Rome, and afk yourfelf (I put the queftion to your heart, and beg you will confult that for an anfwer, afk yourfelf) whether her abfurd pretenfions to that very kind of miraculous powers, you have here difplayed as operating to the increafe of Chriftianity, have not converted half her numbers to Proteftantifm, and the other half to Infidelity? Neither the fword of the civil magiftrate, nor the poffeffion of the keys

of

of heaven, nor the terrors of her fpiritual thunder, have been able to
keep within her pale, even thofe who
have been bred up in her faith, how
then fhould you think, that the very
caufe which hath almoft extinguifhed
Chriftianity among Chriftians, fhould
have eftablifhed it among Pagans ?
I beg I may not be mifunderftood, I
do not take upon me to fay, that all
the miracles recorded in the hiftory of
the primitive church after the apoftolical age, were forgeries, it is foreign
to the prefent purpofe to deliver any
opinion upon that fubject; but I do
beg leave to infift upon this, that
fuch of them as were forgeries, muft
in that learned age, by their eafy de-
tection, have rather impeded than
accelerated the progrefs of Chriftianity : and it appears very probable
to

3

) me, that nothing but the recent
prevailing evidence of real, unquef-
tioned, apoftolical miracles, could
have fecured the infant church from
being deftroyed by thofe which were
falfely afcribed to it.

It is not every man who can nicely
feparate the corruptions of religion
from religion itfelf; nor juftly ap-
portion the degrees of credit due
to the diverfities of evidence; and
thofe who have ability for the tafk,
are ufually ready enough to eman-
cipate themfelves from gofpel re-
ftraints (which thwart the propen-
fities of fenfe, check the ebullitions
of paffion, and combat the prejudices
of the world at every turn) by blend-
ing its native fimplicity with the fuperftitions which have been derived

from

from it. No argument so well suited
to the indolence or the immorality
of mankind, as that priests of all ages
and religions are the same, we see
the pretensions of the Romish priefthood to miraculous powers, and we
know them to be falfe; we are confcious, that they at leaft muft facri-
fice their integrity to their intereft,
or their ambition, and being perfuaded, that there is a great fame-
nefs in the paffions of mankind, and
in their incentives to action, and
knowing, that the hiftory of paft ages
is abundantly ftored with fimilar
claims to fupernatural authority, we
traverfe back in imagination the moft
diftant regions of antiquity; and
finding, from a fuperficial view, nothing to difcriminate one fet of men,
or one period of time from another,
we

we haftily conclude, that all revealed religion is a cheat, and that the miracles attributed to the Apoftles themfelves are fupported by no better teftimony, nor more worthy our attention, than the prodigies of Pagan ftory, or the lying wonders of Papal artifice I have no intention, in this place, to enlarge upon the many circumftances, by which a candid enquirer after truth might be enabled to diftinguifh a pointed difference between the miracles of Chrift and his Apoftles, and the tricks of ancient or modern fuperftition. One obfervation I would juft fuggeft to you upon the fubject, the miracles recorded in the Old and New Teftament are fo intimately united with the narration of common events, and the ordinary tranfactions of life, that you

E   cannot,

cannot, as in profane history, separate the one from the other. M
meaning will be illuftrated by an inftance . Tacitus and Suetonius have
handed down to us an account of
many great actions performed by
Vefpafian; amongft the reft, they
inform us of his having wrought fome
miracles, of his having cured a lame
man, and reftored fight to one that
was blind. But what they tell us of
thefe miracles, is fo unconnected
with every thing that goes before and
after, that you may reject the relation of them without injuring, in any
degree, the confiftency of the narration of the other circumftances of
his life : on the other hand, if you
reject the relation of the miracles faid
to have been performed by Jefus
Chrift, you muft neceffarily reject
the

the account of his whole life, and of feveral tranfactions, concerning which we have the undoubted teftimony of other writers befides the Evangelifts. But if this argument fhould not ftrike you, perhaps the following obfervation may tend to remove a little of the prejudice ufually conceived againft gofpel miracles, by men of lively imaginations, from the grofs forgeries attributed to the firft ages of the church.

The phænomena of phyfics are fometimes happily illuftrated by an hypothefis; and the moft recondite truths of mathematical fcience not unfrequently inveftigated from an abfurd pofition : what if we try the fame method of arguing in the cafe before us? Let us fuppofe then, that a new

E 2 　　　　　reve-

revelation was to be promulged to mankind, and that twelve unlearned and unfriended men, inhabitants of any country moſt odious and deſpicable in the eyes of Europe, ſhould by the power of God be endowed with the faculty of ſpeaking languages they had never learned, and performing works ſurpaſſing all human ability; and that being ſtrongly impreſſed with a particular truth, which they were commiſſioned to promulgate, they ſhould travel not only through the barbarous regions of Africa, but through all the learned and poliſhed ſtates of Europe; preaching every where with unremitted ſedulity a new religion, working ſtupendous miracles in atteſtation of their miſſion, and communicating to their firſt converts (as a

ſeal

feal of their converfion) a variety of fpiritual gifts, does it appear probable to you, that after the death of thefe men, and probably after the deaths of moft of their immediate fucceffors, who had been zealoufly attached to the faith they had feen fo miraculoufly confirmed, that none would ever attempt to impofe upon the credulous or the ignorant, by a fictitious claim to fupernatural powers? would none of them afpire to the gift of tongues? would none of them miftake phrenzy for illumination, and the delufions of a heated brain for the impulfes of the fpirit? would none undertake to cure inveterate diforders, to expel demons, or to raife the dead? As far as I can apprehend, we ought, from fuch a pofition, to deduce, by every rule

of

of probable reasoning, the precise conclusion, which was in fact verified in the case of the Apostles; every species of miracles, which heaven had enabled the first preachers to perform, would be counterfeited, either from misguided zeal or interested cunning, either through the imbecility or the iniquity of mankind; and we might just as reasonably conclude, that there never was any piety, charity, or chastity in the world, from seeing such plenty of pretenders to these virtues, as that there never were any real miracles performed, from considering the great store of those which have been forged.

But, I know not how it has happened, there are many in the present

sent age (I am far from including you, Sir, in the number) whose prejudices against all miraculous events have arisen to that height, that it appears to them utterly impossible for any human testimony, however great, to establish their credibility. I beg pardon for styling their reasoning, prejudice; I have no design to give offence by that word; they may, with equal right, throw the same imputation upon mine; and I think it just as illiberal in divines, to attribute the scepticism of every Deist to wilful infidelity; as it is in the Deists, to refer the faith of every divine to professional bias. I have not had so little intercourse with mankind, nor shunned so much the delightful freedom of social converse,

E 4

as

as to be ignorant, that there are
many men of upright morals and
good underftandings, to whom, as
you exprefs it, " a latent and even
involuntary fcepticifm adheres;" and
who would be glad to be perfuaded
to be Chriftians : and how fevere
foever fome men may be in their
judgments concerning one another;
yet we Chriftians, at leaft, hope and
believe, that the great Judge of all
will make allowance for " our habits of ftudy and reflection," for various circumftances, the efficacy of
which, in giving a particular bent to
the underftandings of men, we can
neither comprehend, nor eftimate.
For the fake of fuch men, if fuch
fhould ever be induced to throw an
hour away in the perufal of thefe letters,

ters, fuffer me to ftep for a moment out of my way, whilft I hazard an obfervation or two upon the fubject.

Knowledge is rightly divided by Mr. Locke into intuitive, fenfitive, and demonftrative. It is clear, that a paft miracle can neither be the object of fenfe nor of intuition, nor confequently of demonftration; we cannot then, philofophically fpeaking, be faid to know, that a miracle has ever been performed. But, in all the great concerns of life, we are influenced by probability rather than knowledge. and of probability, the fame great author eftablifhes two foundations, a conformity to our own experience, and the teftimony of others. Now it is contended, that by the oppofition of

E 5   thefe

thefe two principles, probability is deftroyed; or, in other terms, that human teftimony can never influence the mind to affent to a propofition repugnant to uniform experience.— Whofe experience do you mean? You will not fay, your own; for the experience of an individual reaches but a little way; and no doubt, you daily affent to a thoufand truths in politics, in phyfics, and in the bufi- nefs of common life, which you have never feen verified by experience.— You will not produce the experience of your friends; for that can extend itfelf but a little way beyond your own.—But by uniform experience, I conceive, you are defirous of un- derftanding the experience of all ages and nations fince the foundation of the world. I anfwer, firft, how is it that you become acquainted with the experience of all ages and nations? You will reply, from history. —Be it fo:—Perufe then by far the moft ancient recoids of antiquity; and if you find no mention of miracles in them, I give up the point. Yes;—but every thing related therein refpecting miracles, is to be reckoned fabulous.——Why?—Becaufe miracles contradict the experience of all ages and nations. Do you not perceive, Sir, that you beg the very queftion in debate? for we affirm, that the great and learned nation of Egypt, that the Heathen inhabiting the land of Canaan, that the numerous people of the Jews, and the nations which, for ages, furiounded them, have all had great experience of miracles. You cannot otherways

E 6   obviate

obviate this conclusion, than by quef-
tioning the authenticity of that book,
concerning which, Newton, when he
was writing his Commentary on Daniel, expreffed himfelf to the perfon ⁂ from whom I had the anec-
dote, and which deferves not to be
loft : " I find more fure marks of
authenticity in the Bible, than in any
profane hiftory whatfoever."

However, I mean not to prefs you
with the argument *ad verecundiam* ; it
is needlefs to folicit your modefty,
when it may be poffible, perhaps, to
make an impreffion upon your judgment : I anfwer, therefore, in the
fecond place, that the admiffion of
the principle by which you reject

* Dr. Smith, late Mafter of Trinity College.

miracles,

miracles, will lead us into abfurdity. The laws of gravitation are the moft obvious of all the laws of nature; every perfon in every part of the globe, muft of neceffity have had experience of them. There was a time when no one was acquainted with the laws of magnetifm, thefe fufpend in many inftances the laws of gravity. nor can I fee, upon the principle in queftion, how the reft of mankind could have credited the teftimony of their firft difcoverer; and yet to have rejected it, would have been to reject the truth. But that a piece of iron fhould afcend gradually from the earth, and fly at laft with an increafing rapidity through the air, and attaching itfelf to another piece of iron, or to a particular fpecies of iron ore, fhould remain fufpended in oppofi-

tion

tion to the action of its gravity, is consonant to the laws of nature.——I grant it; but there was a time when it was contrary, I say not to the laws of nature, but to the uniform experience of all preceding ages and countries; and at that particular point of time, the testimony of an individual, or of a dozen individuals, who should have reported themselves eye witnesses of such a fact, ought, according to your argumentation, to have been received as fabulous. And what are those laws of nature, which, you think, can never be suspended? are they not different to different men, according to the diversities of their comprehension and knowledge? and if any one of them (that, for instance, which rules the operations of magnetism or electri-

electricity) fhould have been known to you or to me alone, whilft all the reft of the world were unacquainted with it, the effects of it would have been new, and unheard of in the annals, and contrary to the experience, of mankind, and therefore ought not, in your opinion, to have been believed. Nor do I underftand what difference, as to credibility, there could be between the effects of fuch an unknown law of nature and a miracle : for it is a matter of no moment, in that view, whether the fufpenfion of the known laws of nature be effected, that is, whether a miracle be performed, by the mediation of other laws that are unknown, or by the miniftry of a perfon divinely commiffioned, fince it is impoffible for us to be certain,

that

that it is contradictory to the consti-
tution of the univerfe, that the laws
of nature, which appear to us general, fhould not be fufpended, and
their action over-ruled by others, ftill
more general, though lefs known;
that is, that miracles fhould not be
performed before fuch a being as
man, at thofe times, in thofe places,
and under thofe circumftances, which
God, in his univerfal providence,
had pre-ordained.

I am, &c.

LETTER FOURTH.

SIR,

I READILY acknowledge the
utility of your fourth caufe, " the
virtues of the firft Chriftians," as
greatly conducing to the fpreading
their religion, but then you feem
to quite mar the compliment you
pay them, by reprefenting their virtues as proceeding either from their
repentance for having been the moft
abandoned finners, or from the lau-
dable defire of fupporting the repu-

tation

tation of the fociety in which they were engaged.

That repentance is the firft ftep to virtue, is true enough, but I fee no reafon for fuppofing, according to the calumnies of Celfus and Julian, " that the Chriftians allured into their party, men who wafhed away in the waters of baptifm the guilt for which the temples of the gods refufed to grant them any expiation." The Apoftles, Sir, did not, like Romulus, open an afylum for debtors, thieves, and murderers ; for they had not the fame fturdy means of fecuring their adherents from the grafp of civil power : they did not perfuade them to abandon the temples of the gods, becaufe they could there obtain no expiation for their guilt, but

but becaufe every degree of guilt was expiated in them with too great facility; and every vice practifed, not only without remorfe of private confcience, but with the powerful fanction of public approbation.

" After the example," you fay, " of their Divine Mafter, the miffionaries of the gofpel addreffed themfelves to men, and efpecially to women, oppreffed by the confcioufnefs, and very often by the effects, of their vices."—This, Sir, I really think, is not a fair reprefentation of the matter; it may catch the applaufe of the unlearned, embolden many a ftripling to caft off for ever the fweet blufh of modefty, confirm many a diffolute veteran in the practice of his impure habits, and fuggeft

great

great occasion of merriment and wanton mockery to the flagitious of every denomination and every age; but still it will want that foundation of truth, which alone can recommend it to the serious and judicious. The Apostles, Sir, were not like the Italian *Fratricelli* of the thirteenth, nor the French *Turlupins* of the fourteenth century; in all the dirt that has been raked up against Christianity, even by the worst of its enemies, not a speck of that kind have they been able to fix, either upon the Apostles, or their Divine Master. The gospel of Jesus Christ, Sir, was not preached in single houses or obscure villages, not in subterraneous caves and impure brothels, not in lazars and in prisons, but in the synagogues and in the temples, in the

streets

ftreets and in the market-places of the great capitals of the Roman provinces, in Jerufalem, in Corinth, and in Antioch, in Athens, in Ephefus, and in Rome. Nor do I any where find that its miffionaries were ordered particularly to addrefs themfelves to the fhamelefs women you mention; I do indeed find the direct contrary, for they were ordered to turn away from, to have no fellowfhip or intercourfe with fuch as were wont *to creep into houfes, and lead cap'tve filly women laden with fins, led away with divers lufts.* And what if a few women, who had either been feduced by their paffions, or had fallen victims to the licentious manners of their age, fhould be found amongft thofe who were moft ready to receive a religion that forbad

bad all impunity? I do not appre
hend that this circumstance ought to
bring an insinuation of discredit, either upon the sex, or upon those who
wrought their reformation.

That the majority of the first converts to Christianity, were of an in-
ferior condition in life, may readily
be allowed; and you yourself have
in another place given a good reafon for it; those who are distin-
guished by riches, honours, or knowledge, being so very inconsiderable
in number, when compared with the
bulk of mankind but though not
many mighty, not many noble were
called, yet some mighty, and some
noble, some of as great reputation as
any of the age in which they lived,
were attached to the Christian faith.

Shor

Short indeed are the accounts, which have been tranfmitted to us, of the firft propagating of Chriftianity; yet even in thefe we meet with the names of many, who would have done credit to any caufe: I will not pretend to enumerate them all; a few of them will be fufficient to make you recollect, that there were, at leaft, fome converts to Chriftianity, both from among the Jews and the Gentiles, whofe lives were not ftained with inexpiable crimes. Amongft thefe we reckon Nicodemus, a ruler of the Jews, Jofeph of Arimathea, a man of fortune and a counfellor; a nobleman and a centurion of Capernaum, Jairus, Crifpus, Softhenes, rulers of fynagogues, Apollos, an eloquent and learned man, Zenas, a Jewifh lawyer, the treafurer of Candace

dace queen of Æthiopia; Cornelius, a centurion of the Italian band, Dionyfius, a member of the Areopagus at Athens; and Sergius Paulus, a man of proconfular or prætorian authority, of whom it may be remarked, that if he refigned his high and lucrative office in confequence of his turning Chriftian, it is a ftrong prefumption in its favour; if he retained it, we may conclude, that the profeffion of Chriftianity was not fo utterly incompatible with the difchaige of the offices of civil life, as you fometimes reprefent it. This catalogue of men of rank, fortune, and knowledge, who embraced Chriftianity, might, was it neceffary, be much enlarged, and probably another converfation with St. Paul would have enabled us to grace it with the names of Feftus,

and

and king Agrippa himfelf: not that
the writers of the Books of the New
Teftament feem to have been at all
folicitous in mentioning the great or
the learned who were converted to
the faith ; had that been part of their
defign, they would, in the true ftyle
of impoftors, have kept out of fight
the publicans and finners, the tanners
and the tentmakers with whom they
converfed and dwelt ; and introduced
to our notice none but thofe who had
been *brought up with Herod, or the*
chief men of Afia—whom they had the
honour to number amongft their
friends.

That the primitive Chriftians took
great care to have an unfullied reputation, by abftaining from the com-
miffion of whatever might tend to

F   pollute

pollute it, is eafily admitted , but we
do not fo eafily grant, that this cate
is a " circumftance which ufually at-
tends fmall affemblies of men, when
they feparate themfelves from the
body of a nation, or the religion to
which they belonged." It did not
attend the Nicolaitanes, the Simo-
nians, the Menandrians, and the Car-
pocratians in the firft ages of the
church, of which you are fpeaking ,
and it cannot be unknown to you,
Sir, that the fcandalous vices of
thefe very early fectaries, brought a
general and undiftinguifhed cenfure
upon the Chriftian name ; and fo far
from promoting the increafe of the
church, excited in the minds of the
Pagans an abhorrence of whatever
refpected it : it cannot be unknown
to you, Sir, that feveral fectaries both

at

at home and abroad might be mentioned, who have departed from the religion to which they belonged; and which, unhappily for themfelves and the community, have taken as little care to preferve their reputation unfpotted, as thofe of the firft and fecond centuries. If then the firft Chriftians did take the care you mention (and I am wholly of your opinion in that point), their folicitude might as candidly, perhaps, and as reafonably be derived from a fenfe of their duty, and an honeft endeavour to difcharge it, as from the mere defire of increafing the honour of their confraternity by the illuftrious integrity of its members.

You are eloquent in defcribing the auftere morality of the primitive

Chrif-

Chriſtians, as adverſe to the propen-
ſities of ſenſe, and abhorrent from
all the innocent pleaſures and amuſe-
ments of life, and you enlarge, with
a ſtudied minuteneſs, upon their cen-
ſures of luxury, and their ſentiments
concerning marriage and chaſtity .——
but in this circumſtantial enumera-
tion of their errors or, their faults
(which I am under no neceſſity of denying or excuſing) you ſeem to forget the very purpoſe for which you
profeſs to have introduced the mention of them, for the picture you
have drawn is ſo hideous, and the
colouring ſo diſmal, that inſtead of
alluring to a cloſer inſpection, it
muſt have made every man of pleaſure or of ſenſe turn from it with hor-
ror or diſguſt, and ſo far from con-
tributing to the rapid growth of
Chriſ-

Chriſtianity by the auſterity of their
manners, it muſt be a wonder to any
one, how the firſt Chriſtians ever
made a ſingle convert.—It was firſt
objected by Celſus, that Chriſtianity
was a mean religion, inculcating
ſuch a puſillanimity and patience under affronts, ſuch a contempt of
riches and worldly honours, as muſt
weaken the nerves of civil government, and expoſe a ſociety of Chriſtians to the prey of the firſt invaders.
This objection has been repeated by
Bayle; and though fully anſwered
by Bernard and others, it is ſtill the
favourite theme of every *eſprit fort*
of our own age. even you, Sir,
think the averſion of Chriſtians to the
buſineſs of war and government,
" a criminal diſregard to the public
welfare." To all that has been ſaid
upon this ſubject, it may with juſtice,

I think,

I think, be anfwered, that Chriftianity troubles not itfelf with order-
ing the conftitutions of civil focie-
ties, but levels the weight of all its
influence at the hearts of the individuals which compofe them, and, as
Origen faid to Celfus, was every individual in every nation a gofpel
Chriftian, there would be neither internal injuftice, nor external war;
there would be none of thofe paffions which embitter the intercourfes
of civil life, and defolate the globe.
What reproach then can it be to a
religion, that it inculcates doctrines
which, if univerfally practifed, would
introduce univerfal tranquillity, and
the moft exalted happinefs amongft
mankind?

It muft proceed from a total mif-
apprehen-

apprehenſion of the deſign of the Chriſtian diſpenſation, or from a very ignorant interpretation of the particular injunctions, forbidding us to make riches or honours a primary purſuit, or the prompt gratification of revenge a firſt principle of action, to infer—that an individual Chriſtian is obliged by his religion to offer his throat to an aſſaſſin, and his property to the firſt plunderer ; or that a ſociety of Chriſtians may not repel, in the beſt manner they are able, the unjuſt aſſaults of hoſtile invaſion.

I know of no precepts in the goſpel, which debar a man from the poſſeſſion of domeſtic comforts, or deaden the activity of his private friendſhips, or prohibit the exertion

F 4

of

of his utmoſt ability in the ſerviæ of the public; the *nſi quietum nihil beatum* is no part of the Chriſtian's Creed. his virtue is an active virtue; and we juſtly refer to the ſchool of Epicurus the doctrines concerning abſtinence from marriage, from the cultivation of friendſhip, from the management of public affairs, as ſuited to that ſelfiſh indolence, which was the favourite tenet of his philoſophy.

I am, &c.

LETTER FIFTH.

SIR,

"THE union and the difcipline of the Chriftian church," or, as you are pleafed to ftyle it, of the Chriftian republic, is the laft of the five fecondary caufes, to which you have referred the rapid and extenfive fpread of Chriftianity. It muft be acknowledged, that union effentially contributes to the ftrength of every affociation, civil, military, and religious, but unfortunately for your argument, and much to the reproach

F 5   of

of Chriftians, nothing has been more wanting amongft them, from the apoftolic age to our own, than union. *I am of Paul, and I of Apollos, and I of Cephas, and I of Chrift*, are expreffions of difunion which we meet with in the earlieft period of church hiftory. and we cannot look into the writings of any, either friend or foe to Chriftianity, but we find the one of them lamenting, and the other exulting in an immenfe catalogue of fectaries; and both of them thereby furnifhing us with great reafon to believe, that the divifions with refpect to doctrine, worfhip, and difcipline, which have ever fubfifted in the church, muft have greatly tended to hurt the credit of Chriftianity, and to alienate the minds of the Gentiles from the reception

ception of fuch a various and difcordant faith.

I readily grant, that there was a certain community of doctrine, an intercourfe of hofpitality, and a confederacy of difcipline eftablifhed amongft the individuals of every church, fo that none could be admitted into any affembly of Chriftians, without undergoing a previous examination into his manner of life⸱ (which fhews, by the bye, that every reprobate could not, as the fit feized him, or his intereft induced him, become a Chriftian), and without pro-

---

' Nonnulli præpofiti funt, qui in vitam et mores eorum, qui admittuntur, inquirant, ut non corceffa facientes candidatos religionis arceant a fuis conventibus.—Orig. con. Celf. Lib. 2.

tefting

testing in the most solemn manner,
that he would neither be guilty of
murder, nor adultery, nor theft, nor
perfidy; and it may be granted also,
that those who broke this compact,
were ejected by common consent
from the confraternity into which
they had been admitted: it may be
further granted, that this confederacy extended itself to independent
churches; and that those who had,
for their immoralities, been exclud-
ed from Christian community in any
one church, were rarely, if ever,
admitted to it by another; just as a
member, who has been expelled any
one College in an University, is generally thought unworthy of being
admitted by any other: but it is not
admitted, that this severity and this
union of discipline could ever have
induced

induced the Pagans to forfake the gods of their country, and to expofe themfelves to the contemptuous hatred of their neighbours, and to all the feverities of perfecution exercifed, with unrelenting barbarity, againft the Chriftians.

The account you give of the origin and progrefs of epifcopal jurifdiction, of the pre-eminence of the Metropolitan churches, and of the ambition of the Roman Pontiff, I believe to be in general accurate and true; and I am not in the leaft furprifed at the bitternefs which now and then efcapes you in treating this fubject: for, to fee the moft benign religion that imagination can form, becoming an inftrument of oppreffion; and the moft humble one adminifterminiſtering to the pride, the avarice, and the ambition of thoſe who wiſhed to be conſidered as its guardians, and who avowed themſelves its pro feſſors, would extort a cenſure from men more attached probably to church authority than yourſelf. not that I think it either a very candid, or a very uſeful undertaking, to be ſolely and induſtriouſly engaged in portraying the characters of the pro feſſors of Chriſtianity in the worſt co-lours, it is not candid, becauſe " the great law of impartiality, which ob-liges an hiſtorian to reveal the im-perfections of the uninſpired teach-ers and believers of the goſpel," obliges him alſo not to conceal, or to paſs over with niggard and reluc-tant mention, the illuſtrious virtues of thoſe, who gave up fortune and fame,

fame, all their comforts, and all their
hopes in this life, nay, life itfelf, rather than violate any one of the precepts of that gofpel, which, from the
teftimony of infpired teachers, they
conceived they had good reafon to
believe, it is not ufeful, becaufe "to
a carelefs obferver" (that is to the
generality of mankind) "*their* faults
may feem to caft a fhade on the faith
which they profeffed,"and may really
infect the minds of the young and
unlearned efpecially, with prejudices
againft a religion, upon their rational
reception or rejection of which, a
matter of the utmoft importance may
(believe me, Sir, it may, for aught
you or any perfon elfe can prove to
the contrary) entirely depend. It is
an eafy matter to amufe ourfelves
and others with the immoralities of

priefts

priefts and the ambition of prelates, with the abfurd virulence of fynods and councils, with the ridiculous doc- trines which vifionary enthufiafts or interefted churchmen have fanctified with the name of Chriftian but a difplay of ingenuity or erudition up- on fuch fubjects is much mifplaced, fince it excites almoft in every per- fon, an unavoidable fufpicion of the purity of the fource itfelf, from which fuch polluted ftreams have been de- rived. Do not miftake my mean- ing; I am far from wifhing, that the clergy fhould be looked up to with a blind reverence, or their imperfec- tions fcreened by the fanctity of their function, from the animadverfion of the world; quite the contrary : their conduct, I am of opinion, ought to be more nicely fcrutinized, and their

devia-

deviation from the rectitude of the gospel more severely censured, than that of other men; but great care should be taken, not to represent *their* vices, or *their* indiscretions, as originating in the principles of their religion. Do not mistake me: I am not here begging quarter for Christianity, or contending, that even the principles of our religion should be received with implicit faith; or that every objection to Christianity should be stifled, by a representation of the mischief it might do, if publicly promulged: on the contrary, we invite, nay, we challenge you to a direct and liberal attack; though oblique glances, and disingenuous insinuations, we are willing to avoid; well knowing, that the character of our religion, like that

of

of an honeſt man, is defended with greater difficulty againſt the ſuggeſt-ions of ridicule, and the ſecret ma-lignity of pretended friends, than againſt poſitive accuſations, and the avowed malice of open enemies.

In your account of the primitive church, you ſet forth, that " the want of diſcipline and human learn-ing was ſupplied by the occaſional aſ-ſiſtance of the prophets ; who were called to that function without dif-tinction of age, of ſex, or of natural abilities."—That the gift of prophe-cy was one of the ſpiritual gifts by which ſome of the firſt Chriſtians were enabled to co-operate with the Apoſtles, in the general deſign of preaching the Goſpel , and that this gift, or rather, as Mr. Locke thinks,

the

the gift of tongues (by the oftenta-
tion of which, many of them were
prompted to fpeak in their affemblies at the fame time), was the occafion of fome diforder in the church
of Corinth, which required the interpofition of the Apoftle to compofe, is
confeffed on all hands. But if you
mean, that the prophets were ever
the fole paftors of the faithful ; or
that no provifion was made by the
Apoftles for the good government
and edification of the church, except
what might be accidentally derived
from the occafional affiftance of the
prophets, you are much miftaken ;
and have undoubtedly forgot what
is faid of Paul and Barnabas having
ordained elders in Lyftra, Iconium,
and Antioch ; and of Paul's com-
miffion to Titus, whom he had left

in Crete, to ordain elders in every city; and of his inftructions both to him and Timothy, concerning the qualifications of thofe whom they were to appoint bifhops; one of which was, that a bifhop fhould be able, by found doctrine, to exhort and to convince the gain-fayer : nor is it faid, that this found doctrine was to be communicated to the bifhop by prophecy, or that all perfons, without diftinction, might be called to that office; but a bifhop was *to be able to teach*, not what he had learned by prophecy, but what Paul had publicly preached; *the things that thou haft heard of me among many witneffes, the fame commit thou to faithful men, who fhall be able to teach others alfo.* And in every place almoft, where prophets are mentioned, they are joined with apoftles and teachers, and other minifters of the gofpel; fo that there is no reafon for your reprefenting them as a diftinct order of men, who were by their occafional affiftance to fupply the want of difcipline and human learning in the church. It would be taking too large a field, to inquire, whether the prophets you fpeak of were endowed with ordinary or extraordinary gifts; whether they always fpoke by the immediate impulfe of the Spirit, or according to *the analogy of faith*, whether their gift confifted in the foretelling of future events, or in the interpreting of fcripture to the edification and exhortation and comfort of the church, or in both: I will content myfelf with obferving, that he will judge very improperly concerning

cerning the prophets of the apoſto-
lic church, who takes his idea of
their office or importance from your
deſcription of them.

In ſpeaking of the community of
goods, which, you ſay, was adopted
for a ſhort time in the primitive
church, you hold as inconcluſive the
arguments of Moſheim; who has
endeavoured to prove, that it was a
community quite different from that
recommended by Pythagoras or Plato; conſiſting principally in a common uſe, derived from an unbound-
ed liberality, which induced the opu-
lent to ſhare their riches with their
indigent brethren : there have been
others, as well as Moſheim, who
have entertained this opinion; and
it is not quite ſo indefenſible as you
repreſent

reprefent it: but whether it be reasonable or abfurd, need not now be examined; it is far more neceffary to take notice of an expreffion which you have ufed, and which may be apt to miflead unwary readers into a very injurious fufpicion, concerning the integrity of the Apoftles. In procefs of time, you obferve, " the converts who embraced the new religion, were permitted to retain the poffeffion of their patrimony."— This expreffion, *permitted to retain,* in ordinary acceptation, implies an antecedent obligation to part with: now, Sir, I have not the fhadow of a doubt in affirming, that we have no account in fcripture of any fuch obligation being impofed upon the converts to Chriftianity, either by Chrift himfelf, or by his Apoftles, or

by

by any other authority; nay, in the very place where this community of goods is treated of, there is an express proof (I know not how your impartiality has happened to overlook it) to the contrary. When Peter was about to inflict an exemplary punishment upon Ananias (not for keeping back a part of the price, as some men are fond of representing it, but) for his lying and hypocrisy, in offering a part of the price of his land, as the whole of it; he said to him, *Whilst it remained* (unsold), *was it not thine own? and after it was sold, was it not in thine own power?* From this account it is evident, that Ananias was under no obligation to part with his patrimony; and, after he had parted with it, the price was in his own power: the Apostle would have *permitted him to retain* the whole,

of

of it, if he had thought fit; though he would not permit his prevarication to go unpunished.

You have remarked, that " the feasts of love, the agapæ, as they were called, conftituted a very pleafing and effential part of public worfhip."----Leſt any one fhould from hence be led to fufpect, that thefe feafts of love, this pleafing part of the public worfhip of the primitive church, refembled the unhallowed meetings of fome impure fectaries of our own times, I will take the liberty to add to your account, a fhort explication of the nature of thefe agapæ. Tertullian, in the 39th chapter of his Apology, has done it to my hands. " The nature of our fupper," fays he, " is indicated by its

name;

name; it is called by a word which,
in the Greek language, fignifies love.
We are not anxious about the ex-
pence of the entertainment; fince
we look upon that as gain, which is
expended with a pious purpofe, in
the relief and refrefhment of all our
indigent.—The occafion of our entertainment being fo honourable,
you may judge of the manner of its
being conducted, it confifts in the
difcharge of religious duties, it admits nothing vile, nothing immodeft.
Before we fit down, prayer is made
to God. The hungry eat as much
as they defire, and every one drinks
as much as can be ufeful to fober
men. We fo feaft, as men who
have their minds impreffed with the
idea of fpending the night in the
worfhip of God; we fo converfe, as

men

5

men who are conscious that the Lord heareth them, &c." Perhaps you may object to this testimony, in favour of the innocence of Christian meetings, as liable to partiality, because it is the testimony of a Christian; and you may, perhaps, be able to pick out, from the writings of this Christian, something that looks like a contradiction of this account: however, I will rest the matter upon this testimony for the present; forbearing to quote any other Christian writer upon the subject, as I shall in a future letter produce you a testimony superior to every objection. You speak too of the agapæ as an essential part of the public worship: this is not according to your usual accuracy; for, had they been essential, the edict of an heathen magistrate

G 2

would

would not have been able to put a
ftop to them : yet Pliny, in his letter to Trajan, exprefsly fays, that
the Chriftians left them off, upon his
publifhing an edict prohibiting affemblies ; and we know that, in the
council of Carthage, in the fourth
century, on account of the abufes
which attended them, they began to
be interdicted, and ceafed almoft
univerfally in the fifth.

I have but two obfervations to
make upon what you have advanced
concerning the feverity of ecclefiaftical penance, the fiift is, that even
you yourfelf do not deduce its inftitution fiom the fcripture, but from
the power which every voluntary fociety has over its own members, and
therefore, howevei extravagant, or

howevei

however abfurd ; however oppofite to the attributes of a commiferating God, or thé feelings of a fallible man, it may be thought, or upon whatever trivial occafion, fuch as that you mention of calumniating a Bifhop, a Prefbyter, or even a Deacon, it may have been inflicted ; Chrift and his Apoftles are not anfwerable foi it. The other is, that it was, of all poffible expedients, the leaft fitted to accomplifh the end for which you think it was introduced, the propagation of Chriftianity. The fight of a penitent humbled by a public confeffion, emaciated by fafting, clothed in fackcloth, proftrated at the dooi of the affembly, and imploring for years together the pardon of his offences, and a re-admiffion into the bofom of the church,

G 3   was

was a much more likely means of
deterring the Pagans from Chriftian
community, than the pious liberality you mention, was of alluring
them into it. This pious liberality,
Sir, would exhauft even your elegant powers of defcription, befoie
you could exhibit it in the amiable
manner it deferves; it is derived
from the *new commandment of loving
one another*; and it has ever been
the diftinguifhing characteriftic of
Chriftians, as oppofed to every other
denomination of men, Jews, Mahometans, or Pagans. In the times of
the Apoftles, and in the firft ages of
the church, it fhewed itfelf in voluntary contributions for the relief of
the poor and the perfecuted, the in-
firm and the unfortunate: as foon as
the church was permitted to have

perma-

permanent poffeffions in land, and
acquired the protection of the civil power, it exerted itfelf in the
erection of hofpitals of every kind;
inftitutions thefe, of charity and
humanity, which were forgotten
in the laws of Solon and Lycurgus; and for even one example
of which, you will, I believe, in
vain exploie the boafted annals of
Pagan Rome. Indeed, Sir, you will
think too injurioufly of this liberality, if you look upon its origin as
fuperftitious; or upon its application
as an artifice of the priefthood, to fe-
duce the indigent into the bofom of
the church : it was the pure and un-
corrupted fruit of genuine Chriftianity.

You are much *furprifed*, and not a

little

little *concerned*, that Tacitus and the younger Pliny have spoken so slightly of the Christian system; and that Seneca and the elder Pliny have not vouchsafed to mention it at all. This difficulty seems to have struck others, as well as yourself; and I might refer you to the conclusion of the second volume of Dr. Lardner's Collection of Ancient Jewish and Heathen Testimonies to the Truth of the Christian Religion, for full satisfaction in this point; but perhaps an observation or two may be sufficient to diminish your surprise.

Obscure sectaries of upright morals, when they separate themselves from the religion of their country, do not speedily acquire the attention of men of letters. The historians are applic-

apprehenfive of depreciating the dig-
nity of their learned labour, and
contaminating their fplendid narration of illuftrious events, by mixing
with it a difgufting detail of religious
combinations; and the philofophers
are ufually too deeply engaged in
abftract fcience, or in exploring the
infinite intricacy of natural appearances, to bufy themfelves with what
they, perhaps haftily, efteem popular
fuperftitions. Hiftorians and philofophers, of no mean reputation,
might be mentioned, I believe, who
were the contemporaries of Luther
and the firft reformers; and who
have paffed over in negligent or contemptuous filence, their daring and
unpopular attempts to fhake the fta-
bility of St. Peter's Chair. Oppofition to the religion of a people muft

become

become general, before it can deferve the notice of the civil magiftrate; and till it does that, it will
moftly be thought below the animadverfion of diftinguifhed writers. This
remark is peculiarly applicable to
the cafe in point. The firft Chriftians, as Chrift had foretold, were
hated of all men for his name's fake:
it was the name itfelf, not any vices
adhering to the name, which Pliny
punifhed; and they were every
where held in exceeding contempt,
till their numbers excited the apprehenfion of the ruling powers. The
philofophers confidered them as enthufiafts, and neglected them; the
priefts oppofed them as innovators,
and calumniated them; the great
overlooked them, the learned defpifed them; and the curious alone,
                                    who

who examined into the foundation
of their faith, believed them. But
the negligence of fome half dozen
of writers (moft of them however
bear incidental teftimony to the
truth of feveral facts refpecting Chriftianity), in not relating circumftan-
tially the origin, the progrefs, and
the pretenfions of a new fect, is a
very infufficient reafon for queftion-
ing, either the evidence of the principles upon which it was built, or
the fupernatural power by which it
was fupported.

The Roman hiftorians, moreover,
were not only culpably incurious
concerning the Chriftians, but unpardonably ignorant of what concerned either them or the Jews: I
fay, unpardonably ignorant, becaufe

the

the means of information were within their reach : the writings of Moses were every where to be had in Greek; and the works of Josephus were published before Tacitus wrote his history; and yet even Tacitus has fallen into great absurdity, and self-contradiction, in his account of the Jews ; and though Tertullian's zeal carried him much too far, when he called him *Mendaciorum loquacissimus*, yet one cannot help regretting the little pains he took to acquire proper information upon that subject. He derives the name of the Jews, by a forced interpolation, from mount Ida in Crete *; and he represents them as

---

* Inclytum in Creta Idam montem, accolas Idæos aucto in barbarum cognomento Judæos vocitari.—Tac. Hist. l. 5. sub init.

abhorring all kinds of images in public worſhip, and yet accuſes them of having placed the image of an Aſs in the holy of holies : and preſently after he tells us, that Pompey, when he profaned the Temple, found the ſanctuary entirely empty. Similar inaccuracies might be noticed in Plutarch, and other writers who have ſpoken of the Jews ; and you yourſelf have referred to an obſcure paſſage in Suetonius, as offering a proof how ſtrangely the Jews and Chriſtians of Rome were confounded with each other. Why then ſhould we think it remarkable, that a few celebrated writers, who looked upon the Chriſtians as an obſcure ſect of the Jews, and upon the Jews as a barbarous and deteſted people, whoſe hiſtory was not worth the peruſal, and who

were

were moreover engaged in the relation of the great events which either occafioned or accompanied the ruin of their eternal empire; why fhould we be furprifed, that men occupied in fuch interefting fubjects, and influenced by fuch inveterate prejudices, fhould have left us but fhort and imperfect defcriptions of the Chriftian fyftem?

" But how fhall we excufe, you fay, the fupine inattention of the Pagan and philofophic world, to thofe evidences, which were prefented by the hand of omnipotence, not to their reafon, but to their fenfes?"— " The laws of nature were perpetually fufpended, for the benefit of the church : but the fages of Greece and Rome turned afide from the aw-

ful

ful fpectacle."—To their fhame be it fpoken, that they did fo—"and purfuing the ordinary occupations of life and ftudy, appeared unconfcious of any alterations in the moral or phyfical government of the world." —To this objection I anfwer, in the firft place, that we have no reafon to believe, that miracles were performed as often as philofophers deigned to give their attention to them; or that, at the period of time you allude to, the laws of nature were *perpetually* fufpended, for the benefit of the church. It may be, that not one of the few heathen writers, whofe books have efcaped the ravages of time, was ever prefent, when a miracle was wrought; but will it follow, becaufe Pliny, or Plutarch, or Galen, or Seneca, or Suetonius, or Tacitus, had

had never feen a miracle, that no
miracles were ever performed? They
indeed were learned and obfervant
men; and it may be a matter of
furprife to us, that miracles fo celebrated, as the friends of Chriftianity
fuppofe the Chriftian ones to have
been, fhould never have been mentioned by them though they had not
feen them; and had an Adrian or a
Vefpafian been the authors of but a
thoufandth part of the miracles
you have afcribed to the primitive
church, more than one probably of
thefe very hiftorians, philofophers as
they were, would have adorned his
hiftory with the narration of them:
for though they turned afide from
the awful fpectacle of the miracles
of a poor defpifed Apoftle—yet they
beheld with exulting complacency,
and

and have related with unfufpecting credulity, the oftentatious tricks of a Roman Emperor. It was not for want of faith in miraculous events, that thefe fages neglected the Chriftian miracles, but for want of candour and impartial examination.

I anfwer, in the fecond place, that in the Acts of the Apoftles we have an account of a great multitude of Pagans of every condition of life, who were fo far from being inattentive to the evidences, which were prefented by the hand of omnipotence to their fenfes, that they contemplated them with reverence and wonder; and forfaking the religion of their anceftors, and all the flattering hopes of worldly profit, reputation, and tranquillity, adhered with aftonifh-

aftonifhing refolution to the profef
fion of Chriftianity. From the conclufion of the Acts, till the time in
which fome of the fages you mention
flourifhed, is a very obfcure part of
church hiftory; yet we are certain
that many of the Pagan, and we have
fome reafon to believe, that not a
few of the philofophic world, during
that period, did not turn afide from
the awful fpectacle of miracles, but faw
and believed: and that a few others
fhould be found, who probably had
never feen, and therefore would not
believe, is furely no very extraordinary circumftance. Why fhould we
not anfwer to objections, fuch as
thefe, with the boldnefs of St. Jerome; and bid Celfus, and Porphyry,
and Julian, and their followers, learn
the illuftrious characters of the men
who

who founded, built up, and adorned the Chriſtian church * ? why ſhould we not tell them, with Arnobius, of the orators, the grammarians, the rhetoricians, the lawyers, the phyſicians, the philoſophers, "who appeared conſcious of the alterations in the moral and phyſical government of the world ;" and, from that conſciouſneſs, forſook the ordinary occupations of life and ſtudy, and at-

---

* Diſcant Celſus, Porphyrius, Julianus, rabidi adverſus Chriſtum canes, diſcant eorum lectatores, qui putant Eccleſiam nullos Philoſophos et eloquentes, nullos habuiſſe Doctores; quanti et quales viri eam fundaverint, extruxerint, ornaverintque; et deſinant fidem noſtram ruſticæ tantum ſimplicitatis arguere, ſuamque notius imperitiam agnoſcant.—Jero. Prœ. Lib. d. Illuſ. Eccl. Scrip.

tached

tached themfelves to the Chriftian
difcipline *?

I anfwer, in the laft place, that the
miracles of Chriftians were falfely
attributed to magic; and were for
that reafon thought unworthy the notice of the writers you have referred
to. Suetonius, in his life of Nero,
calls the Chriftians, men of a new
and magical fuperftition † : I am fenfible that you laugh at thofe " faga-
cious commentators," who tranflate
the original word by magical; and
adopting the idea of Mofheim, you
think it ought to be rendered mif-

* Arnob. con. Gen. l. 11.

† Genus hominum fuperftitionis no.æ et
maleficæ.—Suet. in Nero. c. 16.

chievou-

chievous or pernicious : unqueftion-
ably it frequently has that meaning;
with due deference, however, to Mofheim and yourfelf, I cannot help
being of opinion, that in this place,
as defcriptive of the Chriftian religion, it is rightly traflated magical.
The Theodofian Code muft be my
excufe, for diffenting from fuch re-
fpectable authority; and in it, I conjecture, you will find good reafon for
being of my opinion *. Nor ought
any friend to Chriftianity to be afto-
nifhed or alarmed at Suetonius ap-
plying the word Magical to the
Chriftian religion; for the miracles

---

* Chaldæi, ac *Magi*, et cæteri quos vulgus
maleficos ob facinorum magnitudinem appellat.
——Si quis *magus* vel magicis contaminibus
adfuetus, qui *maleficus* vulgi confuetudine nun-
cupatur. ix Cod. Theodof. tit. xvi.

wrought

wrought by Chrift and his Apoftle; principally confifted in alleviating the diftreffes, by curing the obftinate difeafes of human kind; and the proper meaning of magic, as underftood by the ancients, is a higher and more holy branch of the ait of healing*. The elder Pliny loft his life in an eruption of Vefuvius, about forty-feven years after the death of Chrift: fome fifteen years before the death of Pliny, the Chriftians were perfecuted at Rome foi a crime, of which

* Pliny, fpeaking of the origin of magic, fays, Natam primum e medicina nemo dubitat, ae fpecie falutari irrepfiffe velut *altiorem fanGio remque medicinam*.—He afterwards fays, that it was mixed with mathematical arts, and thus *magici* and *mathematici* are joined by Pliny, as *malefici* and *magici* are in the Theodofian Code. Plin. Nat. Hift. lib. 30. c. 1.

every

every perfon knew them innocent;
but from the defcription, which Tacitus gives, of the low eftimation
they were held in at that time (for
which, however, he affigns no caufe;
and therefore we may reafonably conjecture it was the fame for which the
Jews were every where become fo
odious, an oppofition to polytheifm),
and of the extreme fufferings they
underwent, we cannot be much furprifed, that their name is not to be
found in the works of Pliny or of
Seneca : the fect itfelf muft, by Nero's perfecution, have been almoft
deftroyed in Rome; and it would
have been uncourtly, not to fay un-
fafe, to have noticed an order of
men, whofe innocence an Emperor
had determined to traduce, in order
to divert the dangerous, but deferved
ftream

ftream of popular cenfure from himfelf. Notwithftanding this, there is
a paffage in the Natural Hiftory of
Pliny, which, how much foever it
may have been overlooked, contains,
I think, a very ftrong allufion to the
Chriftians; and clearly intimates, he
had heard of their miracles. In
fpeaking concerning the origin of
magic, he fays—there is alfo another
faction of magic, derived from the
Jews, Mofes and Lotopea, and fubfifting at prefent *.—The word faction does not ill denote the opinion

* Eft et alia magices *facto*, a Mofe *etiamnum*
et Lotopea Judæis pendens. Plin. Nat. Hift.
lib. 30. c. 2. Edit. Hardu.—Dr. Lardner
and others have made flight mention of this
paffage, probably from their reading in bad editions *Jamne* for *etiamnum*, a Mofe et Jamne et
Jotape Judæis pendens.

the

the Romans entertained of the religious affociations of the Chriftians *, and a magical faction implies their pretenfions, at leaft, to the miraculous gifts of healing, and its defcending from Mofes, is according to the cuftom of the Romans, by which they confounded the Chriftians with the Jews, and its being then fubfifting, feems to have a ftrong reference to the rumours Pliny had negligently heard reported of the Chriftians.

Submitting each of thefe anfwers to your cool and candid confideration, I proceed to take notice of another difficulty in your fifteenth

* Tertullian reckons the fect of the Chriftians, inter licitas *factiones*. Ap. c. 38.

H chapter,

chapter, which fome have though
one of the moft important in your
whole book—The filence of profane
hiftorians, concerning the preternatural darknefs at the crucifixion of
Chrift.—You know, Sir, that feveral learned men are of opinion, that
profane hiftory is not filent upon
this fubject, I will, however, put
their authority for the prefent quite
out of the queftion. I will neither
trouble you with the teftimony of
Phlegon, nor with the appeal of
Tertullian to the public regifters of
the Romans; but meeting you upon
your own ground, and granting you
every thing you defire, I will endeavour, from a fair and candid examination of the hiftory of this event, to
fuggeft a doubt, at leaft, to your
mind, whether this was " the greateft
phæno-

phænomenon, to which the mortal eye has been witnefs, fince the creation of the globe."

This darknefs is mentioned by three of the four Evangelifts, St. Matthew thus expreffes himfelf.— *Now from the fixth hour there was darknefs over all the land until the ninth hour*; St. Mark fays—*And when the fixth hour was come, there was darknefs over the whole land until the ninth hour*; St. Luke—*And it was about the fixth hour, and there was darknefs over all the earth until the ninth hour; and the fun was darkened.* The three Evangelifts agree, that there was darknefs;—and they agree in the extent of the darknefs : for it is the fame expreffion in the original, which our tranflators have rendered *earth* in

Luke,

Luke, and *land* in the two other accounts; and they agree in the duration of the darkneſs, it laſted three hours ·—Luke adds a particular circumſtance, *that the ſun was darkened*. I do not know whether this event be any where elſe mentioned in ſcripture, ſo that our inquiry can neither be extenſive nor difficult.

In philoſophical propriety of ſpeech, darkneſs conſiſts in the total abſence of light, and admits of no degrees ; however, in the more common acceptation of the word, there are degrees of darkneſs, as well as of light ; and as the Evangeliſts have ſaid nothing, by which the particular degree of darkneſs can be determined, we have as much reaſon to ſuppoſe it was ſlight, as you have that

it

it was exceffive; but if it was flight, though it had extended itfelf over the furface of the whole globe, the difficulty of its not being recorded by Pliny or Seneca vanifhes at once *. Do you not perceive, Sir, upon what a flender foundation this mighty objection is grounded; when we have only to put you upon proving, that the darknefs at the cruci-

* The author of L'Evangile de la Raifon is miftaken in faying, that the Evangelifts fpeak of a *thick darknefs*, and that miftake has led him into another, into a difbelief of the event, becaufe it has not been mentioned by the writers of the times—Ces hiftoriens (the Evangelifts) ont le front de nous dire, qu'à fa mort la terre a été couverte d'épaiffes ténèbres en plein midi et en pleine lune, comme fi tous les écrivains de ce tems-là n'auroient pas remarqué un fi étrange miracle '—L'Evan. de la Raif. p 99.

H 3

fixion

fixion was of fo unufual a nature, as
to have excited the particular attention of all mankind, or even of thofe
who were witneffes to it ? But I do
not mean to deal fo logically with
you; rather give me leave to fpare
you the trouble of your proof, by
proving, or fhewing the probability
at leaft, of the direct contrary.
There is a circumftance mentioned
by St. John, which feems to indicate, that the darknefs was not fo exceffive, as is generally fuppofed, for
it is probable that, during the continuance of the darknefs, Jefus fpoke
both to his mother, and to his beloved difciple, whom he *faw* from
the crofs, they were near the crofs,
but the foldiers which furrounded it
muft have kept them at too great a
diftance, for Jefus to have *feen* them
and

and *known* them, had the darkneſs at the crucifixion been exceſſive, like the preternatural darkneſs which God brought upon the land of Egypt; for it is expreſsly ſaid that, during the continuance of that darkneſs, *they ſaw not one another.* The expreſſion in St. Luke, *the ſun was darkened,* tends rather to confirm than to overthrow this reaſoning. I am ſenſible this expreſſion is generally thought equivalent to another—the ſun was eclipſed,—but the Bible is open to us all, and there can be no preſumption in endeavouring to inveſtigate the meaning of ſcripture for ourſelves. Luckily for the preſent argumentation, the very phraſe of the ſun's being darkened, occurs, in ſo many words, in one other place (and in only one) of the New Teſta-

H 4   ment,

ment; and from that place you may possibly fee reafon to imagine, that the darknefs might not, perhaps, have been fo intenfe as to deferve the particular notice of the Roman naturalifts.—*And he opened the bottomlefs pit, and there arofe a fmoke out of the pit, as the fmoke of a great furnace; and the fun was darkened*, and the air, by reafon of the fmoke of the pit.* If we fhould fay, that the fun at the crucifixion was obnubilated, and darkened by the intervention of clouds, as it is here reprefented to be by the intervention of a fmoke like the fmoke of a furnace, I do not fee what you could object to our account; but fuch a phænomenon has furely no right to be efteemed the

* —— και εσκοτισθη ὁ ἡλιος. Ατον. 9 2.

greatest

greateſt that mortal eye has ever beheld. I may be miſtaken in this interpretation; but I have no deſign to
miſrepreſent the fact, in order to get
rid of a difficulty, the darkneſs may
have been as intenſe as many commentators have ſuppoſed it. but neither they nor you can prove it was ſo;
and I am ſurely under no neceſſity,
upon this occaſion, of granting you,
out of deference to any commenta-
tor, what you can neither prove nor
render probable.

But you ſtill, perhaps, may think,
that the darkneſs, by its extent, made
up for this deficiency in point of intenſeneſs. The original word, ex-
preſſive of its extent, is ſometimes
interpreted by the whole earth; more
frequently, in the New Teſtament, of

H 5   any

any little portion of the earth: for we read of the land of Judah, of the land of Ifrael, of the land of Zabulon, and of the land of Nephthalim; and it may very properly, I conceive, be tranflated in the place in queftion by *region*. But why fhould all the world take notice of a darknefs which extended itfelf for a few miles about Jerufalem, and lafted but three hours? The Italians, efpecially, had no reafon to remark the event as fingular, fince they were accuftomed at that time, as they are at prefent, to fee the *neighbouring regions* fo darkened for days together by the eruptions of Ætna and Vefuvius, that no man could know his neighbour [*]. We learn from the fcrip-

---

[*] —— nos autem tenebras cogitemus tantas,

ſcripture account, that an earthquake accompanied this darkneſs; and a dark clouded ſky, I apprehend, very frequently precedes an earthquake; but its extent is not great, nor is its intenſeneſs exceſſive, nor is the phænomenon itſelf, ſo unuſual, as not commonly to paſs unnoticed in ages of ſcience and hiſtory. I fear I may be liable to miſrepreſentation in this place; but I beg it may be obſerved, that however ſlight in degree, or however confined in extent the darkneſs at the crucifixion may have been; I am of opinion, that the

tas, qvantæ quondam eruptione Etnæorum ignium *finitimas regiones obſuraviſſe* dicuntur, ut per biduum nemo hominem homo agnoſceret. Cic de Nat. Deo. l. 2.—And Pliny, in deſcribing the eruption of Veſuvius which ſuffocated his uncle, ſays—Dies alibi, illic nox omnibus noctibus nigrior denſiorque.

power of God was as fupernaturally exerted in its production and in that of the earthquake which accompanied it, as in the opening of the graves, and the refurrection of the faints, which followed the refurrection of Chrift.

In another place, you feem not to believe " that Pontius Pilate informed the Emperor of the unjuft fentence of death, which he had pronounced againft an innocent perfon." And the fame reafon which made him filent as to the death, ought, one would fuppofe, to have made him filent as to the miraculous events which accompanied it : and if Pilate, in his difpatches to the Emperor, tranfmitted no account of the darknefs (how great foever you fuppofe

5   pofe

pofe it to have been) which happened in a diftant province; I cannot
apprehend, that the repoit of it
could have ever gained fuch ciedit
at Rome, as to induce either Pliny
or Seneca to mention it as an authentic fact.

I am, &c.

LETTER SIXTH.

SIR,

I MEAN not to detain you long
with my remarks upon your six-
teenth Chapter; for in a short Apology for Christianity, it cannot be expected that I should apologize at
length for the indiscretions of the
first Christians. Nor have I any dif-
position to reap a malicious pleasure
from exaggerating, what you have
had so much good-natured pleasure

in extenuating, the truculent barba-
uity of their Roman perfecutors.

M. de Voltaire has embraced
every opportunity of contrafting the
perfecuting temper of the Chriftians
with the mild tolerance of the ancient heathens, and I never read a
page of his upon this fubject without
thinking Chriftianity materially, if
not intentionally, obliged to him, for
his endeavour to deprefs the lofty
fpirit of religious bigotry. I may
with juftice pay the fame compliment to you, and I do it with fince-
rity; heartily wifhing that, in the
profecution of your work, you may
render every fpecies of intolerance
univerfally deteftable. There is no
reafon why you fhould abate the
afperity of your invective, fince no
one

one can fufpect you of a defign to
traduce Chriftianity, under the guife
of a zeal againft perfecution, or if
any one fhould be fo fimple, he need
but open the gofpel to be convinced,
that fuch a fcheme is too palpably
abfurd to have ever entered the head
of any fenfible and impartial man.

I wifh, for the credit of human nature, that I could find reafon to agree
with you in what you have faid of the
" univerfal toleration of Polytheifm;
of the mild indifference of antiquity;
of the Roman Princes beholding,
without concern, a thoufand forms
of religion fubfifting in peace under
their gentle fway." But there are
fome paffages in the Roman Hiftory,
which make me hefitate at leaft in
this point; and almoft induce me to
believe

believe that the Romans were exceedingly jealous of all foreign religions, whether they were accompanied with immoral manners or not.

It was the Roman cuſtom, indeed, to invite the tutelary gods of the nations which they intended to ſubdue, to abandon their charge; and to promiſe them the ſame, or even a more auguſt worſhip in the city of Rome *; and their triumphs were graced as much with the exhibition of their captive gods, as with the leſs

* In oppugnationibus, ante omnia ſolitum a Romanis ſacerdotibus evocari deum cujus in tutela id oppidum eſſet; promittique illi eundem, aut ampliorem apud Romanos cultum. Plin. Nat. Hiſt. l. 38. c. iv.

humane

humane one of their captive kings *. But this cuſtom, though it filled the city with hundreds of gods of every country, denomination and quality, cannot be brought a proof of Roman toleration, it may indicate the exceſs of their vanity, the extent of their ſuperſtition, or the refinement of their policy, but it can never ſhew that the religion of individuals, when it differed from public wiſdom, was either connived at as a matter of indifference, or tolerated as an inalienable right of human nature.

Upon another occaſion, you, Sir,

* Roma triumphantis quotiens Ducis inclita currum
Plauſibus excepit, totiens altaria Divûm
Addidit ſpoliis ſibimet nova numina fecit.
Pruden.

have

have referred to Livy as relating the introduction and suppression of the rites of Bacchus; and in that very place we find him confessing, that the prohibiting all foreign religions, and the abolishing every mode of sacrifice which differed from the Roman mode, was a business frequently entrusted by their ancestors to the care of the proper magistrates; and he gives this reason for the procedure · That nothing could contribute more effectually to the ruin of religion, than the sacrificing after an external rite, and not after the manner instituted by their fathers *.

Not

* Quoties hoc patrum avorumque ætate negotium eſt magiſtratibus datum, ut ſacra externa fieri vetarent ? ſacrificulos vateſque foro, circo, urbe prohiberent ? *vaticinos libros conquirerent*

Not thirty years before this event, the Prætor, in conformity to a decree of the senate, had issued an edict—that no one should presume to sacrifice in any public place after a new or foreign manner *. And in a still more early period, the Ædiles had been commanded to take care, that no gods were worshipped except the Roman gods ; and that the Ro-

rent comburerentque ? omnem disciplinam sacri ficandi, præterquam more Romano, abolerent? Judicabant enim prudentissimi viri omnis divini humanique juris, nihil æque dissolvendæ religionis esse, quam ubi non patrio, sed externo ritu sacrificaretur.—Liv. l. xxxix. c. xvi.

* Ut quicumque *libros vaticinos precationesv*, aut artem sacrificandi conscriptam haberet, eos libros omnes litterasque ad se ante Kalendas Apriles deferret neu quis in publico sacrove loco, novo aut externo ritu sacrificaret. Li. L. xxv. c. 1.

man

man gods were worſhipped after no manner but the eſtabliſhed manner of the country *.

But to come nearer to the times of which you are writing. In Dion Caſſius you may meet with a great courtier, one of the interior cabinet, and a poliſhed ſtateſman, in a ſet ſpeech upon the moſt momentous ſubject, expreſſing himſelf to the Emperor, in a manner agreeable enough to the practice of antiquity, but utterly inconſiſtent with the moſt remote idea of religious toleration. The ſpeech alluded to, contains, I

* Datum inde negotium ædilibus, ut animad-verterent, ne qui, niſi Romani dii, neu quo alio more quam patrio, colerentur.—Liv. l. iv. c. 30.

confeſs

confefs it, nothing more than the ad
vice of an individual; but it ought
to be remembered, that *that* indivi
dual was Mæcenas, that the advice
was given to Auguftus, and that the
occafion of giving it was no lefs im
portant than the fettling the form of
the Roman government. He re
commends it to Cæfar, to worfhip
the gods himfelf according to the
eftablifhed form, and to *force* all
others to do the fame; and to *hate*
and to *punifh* all thofe who fhould
attempt to introduce foreign reli
gions *: nay, he bids him, in the
fame place, have an eye upon the

* Ταυ-α τε ετω πραττε, και προσετ. το μ. . θτι
πα.τη παντω, αυτος τε σ-βε, κατα τα πατρια, και
τες αλλες τιμαν αναγκαζε τες δε δη ξειιζοιτας τι πι .
ευτο και μισει και κολαζε. Dion. Caf. l. 52.

philofo-

7

philofophers alfo; fo that free thinking, free fpeaking at leaft, upon religious matters, was not quite fo fafe
under the gentle fway of the Roman
princes, as, thank God, it is under
the much more gentle government
of our own.

In the Edict of Toleration pub-
lifhed by Galerius after fix years unremitted perfecution of the Chriftians, we perceive his motive for
perfecution to have been the fame
with that which had influenced the
conduct of the more ancient Romans, an abhorrence of all innova-
tions in religion. You have favoured us with the tranflation of this
edict, in which he fays—"we were
particularly defirous of reclaiming
into the way of reafon and nature,"

ad

ad bonas mentes (a good pretence this
for a Polytheiſtic perſecutor) " the
deluded Chriſtians who had re-
nounced the religion and ceremo
nies inſtituted by their fathers"—
this is the preciſe language of Livy,
deſcribing a perſecution of a foreign
religion three hundred years before,
*turba erat nec ſacrificantium nec precan-
tium Deos patrio more.* And the very
expedient of forcing the Chriſtians
to deliver up their religious books,
which was practiſed in this perſecution, and which Moſheim attributes
to the advice of Hierocles, and you
to that of the philoſophers of thoſe
times, ſeems clear to me, from the
places in Livy before quoted, to
have been nothing but an old piece
of ſtate policy, to which the Romans had recourſe as often as they
appre-

apprehended their eftablifhed religion to be in any danger.

In the preamble of the letter of
toleration, which the emperor Max-
imin reluctantly wrote to Sabinus
about a year after the publication of
Galerius' Edict, there is a plain
avowal of the reafons which induced
Galerius and Diocletian to commence
their perfecution ; they had feen the
temples of the gods forfaken, and
were determined by the feverity of
punifhment to reclaim men to their
worfhip *.

* Συνειδον σχεδον απαντας ανθρωπης, ν̀αταλειφθειισης
τη. των θεων θρησκεια , τω εθνει των Χριςιανων εαυτης
συμμεμιχοτας. Ορθω, διατεταχεναι παντας αιθρω-
τη, ͂ης απο των θεων των αθανατων αναχωρησαιτας,
τρο δηλω κολασει και τιμωρια εις την θρησκεια, των
θεων ανακληθηναι. Eufeb. lib. ix. c. 4.

In fhort, the fyftem recommended by Mæcenas, of forcing every per-fon to be of the emperor's religion, and of hating and punifhing every innovator, contained no new doc-trine, it was correfpondent to the practice of the Roman fenate, in the moft illuftrious times of the republic; and feems to have been generally adopted by the emper-ors, in their treatment of Chrif-tians, whilft they themfelves were Pagans; and in their treatment of Pagans, after they themfelves be-came Chriftians; and if any one fhould be willing to derive thofe laws againft Heretics (which are fo ab-horrent from the mild fpirit of the gofpel, and fo reproachful to the Roman code) from the blind adhe-

rence

rence of the Chriſtian emperors to
the intolerant policy of their Pagan
predeceſſors, ſomething, I think,
might be produced in ſupport of his
conjecture.

But I am ſorry to have ſaid ſo
much upon ſuch a ſubject.—In endeavouring to palliate the ſeverity of
the Romans towards the Chriſtians,
you have remarked, " it was in vain,
that the oppreſſed believer aſſerted
the inalienable rights of conſcience
and private judgment." " Though
his ſituation might excite the pity,
his arguments could never reach the
underſtanding, either of the philo-
ſophic, or of the believing part of
the Pagan world." How is this, Sir?
are the arguments for liberty of conſcience ſo exceedingly inconcluſive,

that

that you think them incapable of reaching the underftanding, even of philofophers ? A captious adverfary would embrace with avidity the opportunity this paffage affords him, of blotting your character with the odious ftain of being a perfecutor ; a ftain, which no learning can wipe out, which no genius or ability can render amiable. I am far from entertaining fuch an opinion of your principles ; but this conclufion feems fairly deducible from what you have faid—that the minds of the Pagans were fo pre-occupied with the notions of forcing, and hating, and punifhing thofe who differed from them in religion, that arguments for the inalienable rights of confcience, which would have convinced yourfelf and every philofopher in Europe,

rope, and ftaggered the refolution of an inquifitor, were incapable of reaching their underftandings, or making any impreffion on their hearts; and you might, perhaps, have fpared yourfelf fome perplexity, in the inveftigation of the motives which induced the Roman emperors to perfecute, and the Roman people to hate the Chriftians, if you had not overlooked the true one, and adopted with too great facility the erroneous idea of the extreme tolerance of Pagan Rome.

The Chriftians, you obferve, were accufed of atheifm :—and it muft be owned that they were the greateft of all atheifts, in the opinion of the polytheifts, for, inftead of Hefiod's thirty thoufand gods, they could not

I 3   be

be brought to acknowledge above
one; and even that one they refufed, at the hazard of their lives,
to blafpheme with the appellation of
Jupiter. But is it not fomewhat fingular, that the pretenfions of the
Chriftians to a conftant intercourfe
with fuperior beings, in the working
of miracles, fhould have been a prin-
cipal caufe of converting to their
faith, thofe who branded them with
the imputation of atheifm?

They were accufed, too, of form-
ing dangerous confpiracies againft
the ftate:—This accufation, you
own, was as unjuft as the preceding:
but there feems to have been a pe-
culiar hardfhip in the fituation of the
Chriftians, fince the very fame men
who thought them dangerous to the

ftate,

ftate, on account of their confpiracies, condemned them, as you have
obferved, for not interfering in its
concerns, for their criminal difre-
gard to the bufinefs of war and government; and for their entertaining
doctrines, which were fuppofed "to
prohibit them from affuming the
character of foldiers, of magiftrates,
and of princes:" men, fuch as thefe,
would have made but poor confpi-
rators.

They were accufed, laftly, of the
moft horrid crimes.—This accufation, it is confeffed, was mere calumny; yet, as calumny is generally
more extenfive in its influence than
truth, perhaps this calumny might
be more powerful in ftopping the
progrefs of Chriftianity, than the vir-

tues

tues of the Chriſtians were in promoting it : and, in truth, Origen ob-
ſerves that the Chriſtians, on account
of the crimes which were maliciouſly
laid to their charge, were held in
ſuch abhorrence, that no one would
ſo much as ſpeak to them. It may
be worth while to remark from him,
that the Jews, in the very beginning
of Chriſtianity, were the authors of
all thoſe calumnies, which Celſus afterwards took ſuch great delight in
urging againſt the Chriſtians, and
which you have mentioned with ſuch
great preciſion *.

It

* Videtur mihi feciſſe idem Celſus, quod Ju-
dæi, qui ſub Chriſtianiſmi initium errorem ſpar-
fere, quaſi ejus ſectæ homines mactati pueri
veſcerentur carnibus, et quod, quoties eis li-
beat operam dare occultis libidinibus, extincto
lumine

It is no improbable fuppofition,
that the clandeftine manner in which
the perfecuting fpirit of the Jews and
Gentiles obliged the Chriftians to
celebrate their Eucharift, together
with the expreffions of eating the
body, and drinking the blood of
Chrift, which were ufed in its inftitution, and the cuftom of imparting a
kifs of charity to each other, and of
calling each other by the appellations
of brother and fifter *, gave occa-

lumine conftupret, quam quifque nactus fuerit.
Quæ falfa et iniqua opinio dudum valdè multos
a religione noftra alienos tenuit; perfuafos,
quod tales fint Chriftiani, et ad hoc temporis
nonnullos fallit, qui ea de caufa Chriftianos
averfantur, ut nec fimplex colloquium cum eis
habere velint.—Orig. con Celf lib. vi.

* The Romans ufed thefe expreffions in fo
impure a fenfe, that Martial calls them Nomina
aequiora.—Lib. II. epig. iv.

fions

fions to their enemies to invent, and induced carelefs obfervers to believe, all the odious things which were faid againft the Chriftians.

You have difplayed at length, in expreffive diction, the accufations of the enemies of Chriftianity, and you have told us of the imprudent defence by which the Chriftians vindicated the purity of their morals; and you have huddled up in a fhort note (which many a reader will never fee) the teftimony of Pliny to their innocence. Permit me to do the Chriftians a little juftice, by producing in their caufe the whole truth.

Between feventy and eighty years after the death of Chrift, Pliny had

occafion to confult the emperor Trajan concerning the mannei in which
he fhould treat the Chriftians; it
feems as if theie had been judicial
proceedings againft them, though
Pliny had nevei happened to attend
any of them. He knew, indeed,
that men weie to be punifhed for being Chriftians, or he would not, as
a fenfible magiftrate, have ieceived
the accufations of legal, much lefs of
illegal, anonymous informers againft
them; nor would he, before he
wrote to the emperoi, have put to
death thofe whom his thieats could
not hinder from peifevering in theii
confeffion, that they were Chriftians.
His harfh manner of pioceeding " in
an office the moft repugnant to his
humanity," had made many apofta-
tize from their profeffion: perfons

of

of this complexion were well fitted
to inform him of every thing they
knew concerning the Chriftians, ac-
cordingly he examined them; but
not one of them accufed the Chriftians of any other crime than of
praying to Chrift, as to fome God,
and of binding themfelves by an
oath, not to be guilty of any wicked-
nefs. Not contented with this information, he put two maid fervants,
which were called minifters, to the
torture; but even the rack could
not extort from the imbecility of the
fex a confeffion of any crime, any
account different from that which
the apoftates had voluntarily given,
not a word do we find of their feaft-
ing upon murdered infants, or of
their mixing in inceftuous commerce.
After all his pains, Pliny pronounced
the

the meal of the Chriſtians to be *pro-miſcuous* and *innocent* : perſons of both ſexes, of all ages, and of every condition, aſſembled promiſcuouſly together : there was nothing for chaſtity to bluſh at, or for humanity to ſhudder at, in theſe meetings, there was no ſecret initiation of proſelytes by abhorred rites; but they eat a promiſcuous meal in Chriſtian charity, and with the moſt perfect innocence *.

What-

---

* —affirmabant autem, hanc fuiſſe ſummam vel culpæ ſuæ, vel erroris, quod eſſent ſoliti ſtato die ante lucem convenire; carmenque Chriſto, quaſi Deo, dicere ſecum invicem; ſeque ſacramento non *in ſcelus* aliquod obſtringere, ſed ne furta, ne latrocinia, ne adulteria committerent, ne fidem fallerent, ne depoſitum appellati abnegarent, quibus peractis, morem ſibi diſcedendi

Whatever faults then the Christians may have been guilty of in
after times; though you could produce to us a thoufand ambitious
prelates of Carthage, or fenfual ones
of Antioch, and blot ten thoufand
pages with the impurities of the
Chriftian clergy; yet at this period,
whilft the memory of Chrift and his
Apoftles was frefh in their minds;
or, in the more emphatic language
of Jerome, " whilft the blood of our
Lord was warm, and recent faith was
fervent in the believers," we have
the greateft reafon to conclude, that
they were eminently diftinguifhed for
the probity and the purity of their

dendi fuiffe, rurfufque coeundi ad capiendum
eibum, *promifcuum* tamen, *et innoxium.*— Plin.
Epif. xcvii. lib. x.

lives.

lives. Had there been but a shadow
of a crime in their affemblies, it muft
have been detected by the induftrious
fearch of the intelligent Pliny; and
it is a matter of real furprife, that no
one of the apoftates thought of pay-
ing court to the governor by a falfe
teftimony, efpecially, as the apoftacy
feems to have been exceeding general: fince the temples, which had
been almoft deferted, began again
to be frequented, and the victims,
for which a little time before fcarce a
purchafer was to be found, began
again every where to be bought up.
This, Sir, is a valuable teftimony in
our favour; it is not that of a de-
claiming apologift, of a deluding
prieft, or of a deluded martyr, of an
orthodox bifhop, or of any " of the
moft pious of men" the Chriftians;

but

but it is that of a Roman magiſtrate, philoſopher, and lawyer; who cannot be ſuppoſed to have wanted inclination to detect the immoralities or the conſpiracies of the Chriſtians, ſince, in his treatment of them, he had ſtretched the authority of his office, and violated alike the laws of his country, and of humanity.

With this teſtimony I will conclude my remarks. for I have no diſpoſition to blacken the character you have given of Nero; or to leſſen the humanity of the Roman magiſtrates; or to magnify the number of Chriſtians, or of martyrs; or to undertake the defence of a few fanatics, who by their injudicious zeal brought ruin upon themſelves, and diſgrace upon their profeſſion. I may

may not probably have convinced
you that you are wrong in any thing
which you have advanced; or that
the authors you have quoted, will
not fupport you in the inferences you
have drawn from their works, or
that Chriflianity ought to be diftinguifhed from its corruptions. yet I
may, perhaps, have had the good
fortune to leffen, in the minds of
others, fome of that diflike to the
Chriflian religion which the perufal
of your book had unhappily excited.
I have touched but upon general to-
pics; for I fhould have wearied out
your patience, to fay nothing of my
readers', or my own, had I enlarged
upon every thing in which I diffent
from you; and a minute examination of your work would, moreover,
have had the appearance of a captious

tious difpofition to defcend into illiberal perfonalities; and might have
produced a certain acrimony of fen-
timent or expreffion, which may be
ferviceable in fupplying the place of
argument, or adding a zeft to a dull
compofition; but has nothing to do
with the inveftigation of truth. Sorry
fhall I be, if what I have written
fhould give the leaft interruption to
the profecution of the great work in
which you are engaged: the world
is now poffeffed of the opinion of us
both upon the fubject in queftion;
and it may, perhaps, be proper for
us both to leave it in this ftate. I
fay not this from any backwardnefs
to acknowledge my miftakes, when
I am convinced that I am in an error, but to exprefs the almoft infu-
perable reluctance which I feel to
the

the bandying abufive argument in public controverfy · it is not, in good truth, a difficult tafk to chaftife the froward petulance of thofe who miftake perfonal invective for reafoning, and clumfy banter for ingenuity; but it is a dirty bufinefs at beft, and fhould never be undertaken by a man of any temper, except when the interefts of truth may fuffer by his neglect. Nothing of this nature, I am fenfible, is to be expected from you; and if any thing of the kind has happened to efcape myfelf, I hereby difclaim the intention of faying it, and heartily with it unfaid.

Will you permit me, Sir, through this channel (I may not, perhaps, have another fo good an opportunity of doing it) to addrefs a few words,

words, not to yourself, but to a set of men who disturb all serious company with their profane declamation against Christianity; and who having picked up in their travels, or the writings of the deists, a few flimsy objections, infect with their ignorant and irreverent ridicule the ingenuous minds of the rising generation?

GENTLEMEN,

Suppose the mighty work accomplished, the cross trampled upon, Chriftianity every where profcribed, and the religion of Nature once more become the religion of Europe; what advantage will you have derived to your country, or to yourfelves, from the exchange ? I know your anfwer—you will have freed the world from the hypocrify of Priefts, and the tyranny of Superftition.—No; you forget that Lycurgus, and Numa, and Odin, and Mango-Copac, and all the great legiflators of ancient and modern ftory, have been of opinion, that the affairs of civil fociety could not well be conducted with-

without *some* religion; you muſt of
neceſſity introduce a prieſthood,
with probably as much hypocriſy,
a religion, with aſſuredly more ſuperſtition, than that which you now
reprobate with ſuch indecent and ill-
grounded contempt. But I will tell
you from what you will have freed
the world; you will have freed it
from its abhorrence of vice, and
fiom every powerful incentive to
virtue; you will, with the religion,
have brought back the depraved
morality of Paganiſm, you will have
robbed mankind of their firm aſſur-
ance of another life; and thereby you
will have deſpoiled them of their
patience, of their humility, of their
charity, of their chaſtity, of all thoſe
mild and ſilent virtues, which (however deſpicable they may appear in
your

your eyes) are the only ones which meliorate and fublime our nature; which Paganifm never knew, which fpring from Chriftianity alone, which do or might conftitute our comfort in this life, and without the poffef-fion of which, another life, if after all there fhould happen to be one, muft (unlefs a miracle be exerted in the alteration of our difpofition) be more vicious and more miferable than this is.

Perhaps you will contend, that the univerfal light of reafon, that the truth and fitnefs of things, are of themfelves fufficient to exalt the na-ture, and regulate the manners of mankind. Shall we never have done with this groundlefs commendation of natural law? Look into the firft

chapter

chapter of Paul's Epistle to the Romans, and you will see the extent of its influence over the Gentiles of those days; or if you dislike Paul's authority, and the manners of antiquity, look into the more admired accounts of modern voyagers; and examine its influence over the Pagans of our own times, over the sensual inhabitants of Otaheitè, over the Cannibals of New Zealand, or the remorseless Savages of America.—But these men are Barbarians. Your law of nature, notwithstanding, extends even to them.—But they have misused their reason:—they have then the more need of, and would be the more thankful for that revelation, which you, with an ignorant and fastidious self-sufficiency, deem useless.—But they might of them-

themselves, if they thought fit, become wise and virtuous.—I answer
with Cicero, *Ut mhil intereft, utrum
nemo valeat, an nemo valere poffit, fic
non intelligo quid interfit, utrum nemo
fit fapiens, an nemo effe poffit.*

These however, you will think,
are extraordinary inftances; and that
we ought not from thefe to take our
meafure of the excellency of the law
of nature, but rather from the civi-
lized ftates of China and Japan, or
from the nations which flourished in
learning and in arts, before Chriftianity was heard of in the world.
You mean to fay, that by the law of
nature, which you are defirous of
fubftituting in the room of the gofpel, you do not underftand thofe
rules of conduct, which an indivi-

K dual,

dual, abstracted from the community, and deprived of the institution of mankind, could excogitate for himself, but such a system of precepts, as the most enlightened men of the most enlightened ages have recommended to our observance Where do you find this system? We cannot meet with it in the works of Stobæus, or the Scythian Anacharsis; nor in those of Plato, or of Cicero; nor in those of the Emperor Antoninus, or the slave Epictetus, for we are persuaded, that the most animated considerations of the πρε-πον, and the *honestum*, of the beauty of virtue, and the fitness of things, are not able to furnish, even a Brutus himself, with permanent principles of action, much less are they able to purify the polluted recesses of

a vitiated heart, to curb the irregula-
rity of appetite, or restrain the impe-
tuosity of passion in common men.
If you order us to examine the works
of Grotius, or Puffendorf, of Burla-
maqui, or Hutchinson, for what you
understand by the law of nature, we
apprehend that you are in a great
error, in taking your notions of natural law, as discoverable by natural
reason, from the elegant systems of it
which have been drawn up by Christian Philosophers; since they have
all laid their foundations, either ta-
citly or expressly, upon a principle
derived from revelation—a thorough
knowledge of the being and attributes of God and even those
amongst yourselves, who, rejecting
Christianity, still continue Theists,
are indebted to revelation (whether

you

you are either aware of, or difpofed
to acknowledge the debt, or not) for
thofe fublime fpeculations concerning the Deity, which you have
fondly attributed to the excellency
of your own unaffifted reafon. If
you would know the real genius of
natural law, and how far it can proceed in the inveftigation or enforce-
ment of moral duties; you muft confult the manners and the writings of
thofe who have never heard of either
the Jewifh or the Chriftian difpenfation, or of thofe other manifefta-
tions of himfelf, which God vouch-
fafed to Adam and to the Patriarchs
before and after the flood. It would
be difficult perhaps any where, to
find a people entirely deftitute of traditionary notices concerning a Deity,
and of traditionary fears or expectations

tations of another life; and the morals of mankind may have, perhaps, been no where quite fo abandoned as they would have been, had they been left wholly to themfelves in thefe points: however, it is a truth which cannot be denied, how much foever it may be lamented, that though the generality of mankind have always had fome faint conceptions of God and his providence; yet they have been always greatly inefficacious in the production of good morality, and highly derogatory to his nature, amongft all the people of the earth, except the Jews and Chriftians; and fome may perhaps be defirous of excepting the Mahometans, who derive all that is good in their *Koran* from Chriftianity.

The

The laws concerning juftice, and the reparation of damages, concerning the fecurity of property, and the performance of contracts, concerning, in fhort, whatever affects the well-being of civil fociety, have been every where underftood with fufficient precifion ; and if you choofe to ftyle Juftinian's code, a code of natural law, though you will err againft propriety of fpeech, yet you are fo far in the right, that natural reafon difcovered, and the depravity of human nature compelled human kind to eftablifh by proper fanctions the laws therein contained ; and you will have moreover Carneades, no mean philofopher, on your fide, who knew of no law of nature different from that which men had inftituted for their common utility, and which

was

was various according to the manners of men in different climates, and change.ble with a change of times in the fame. And in truth, in all countries where Paganifm has been the eftablifhed religion, though a philofopher may now and then have ftepped beyond the paltry prefcript of civil jurifprudence in his purfuit of virtue , yet the bulk of mankind have ever been contented with that fcanty pittance of morality which enabled them to efcape the lafh of civil punifhment : I call it a fcanty pittance, becaufe a man may be intemperate, iniquitous, impious, a thoufand ways a profligate and a villain, and yet elude the cognizance, and avoid the punifhment of civil laws.

I am

I am fenfible, you will be ready
to fay, what is all this to the purpofe? Though the bulk of mankind
may never be able to inveftigate the
laws of natural religion, nor difpofed
to reverence their fanctions when inveftigated by others, nor folicitous
about any other ftandard of moral
rectitude than civil legiflation; yet
the inconveniences which may attend
the extirpation of Chriftianity can be
no proof of its truth :—I have not
produced them as a proof of its truth;
but they are a ftrong and conclufive
proof, if not of its truth, at leaft of
its utility; and the confideration of
its utility may be a motive to yourfelves for examining, whether it may
not chance to be true; and it ought
to be a reafon with every good citi-
zen, and with every man of found
judgment, to keep his opinions to
himfelf,

himfelf, if, from any particular circumftances in his ftudies or in his
education, he fhould have the mif-
fortune to think that it is not true.
If you can difcover to the rifing generation a better religion than the
Chriftian, one that will more effectually animate their hopes, and fub-
due their paffions, make them better men or better members of fociety, we importune you to publifh
it for their advantage; but till you
can do that, we beg of you not to
give the reins to their paffions, by in-
ftilling into their unfufpicious minds
your pernicious prejudices. Even
now, men fcruple not, by their law-
lefs luft, to ruin the repofe of private
families, and to fix a ftain of infamy
upon the nobleft: even now, they
hefitate not in lifting up a murder-

K 5   ous

ous arm againſt the life of then fiiend, or againſt their own, as often as the fever of intempeiance ſtimulates their reſentment, or the ſatiety of an uſeleſs life excites then deſpondency : even now, whilſt we are perſuaded of a ieſurrection fiom the dead, and of a *judgment to come*, we find it difficult enough to reſiſt the ſolicitations of ſenſe, and to eſcape unſpotted from the licentious manneis of the world : but what will become of our viitue, what of the conſequent peace and happineſs of ſociety, if you perſuade us that theic are no ſuch things? In two words— you may iuin yourſelves by your at tempt, and you will ceitainly iuin your countiy by youi ſucceſs.

But the conſideration of the inutility

tility of your defign, is not the only
one which fhould induce you to
abandon it, the argument *a tuto*
ought to be warily managed, or it
may tend to the filencing our oppofition to any fyftem of fuperftition,
which has had the good fortune to
be fanctified by public authority it
is, indeed, liable to no objection in
the prefent cafe; we do not, however, wholly rely upon its cogency.
It is not contended, that Chriftianity
is to be received merely becaufe it is
ufeful, but becaufe it is true. This
you deny, and think your objections
well grounded we conceive them
originating in your vanity, your immorality, or your mifapprehenfion.
There are many worthlefs doctrines,
many fuperftitious obfervances, which
the fraud or folly of mankind have

every

every where annexed to Chriſtianity (eſpecially in the church of Rome), as eſſential parts of it. if you take theſe ſorry appendages to Chriſtianity for Chriſtianity itſelf, as preached by Chriſt, and by the apoſtles; if you confound the Roman with the Chriſtian religion, you quite miſapprehend its nature, and are in a ſtate ſimilar to that of men mentioned by Plutarch, in his Treatiſe of Superſtition; who, flying from ſuperſtition, leapt over religion, and ſunk into downright Atheiſm *.—Chriſtianity is not a re-ligion

---

* Le Papiſme (ſays Helvetius in a poſt-humous work) n'eſt aux yeux d'un homme ſenſe qu' une pure idolatrie—nous ſommes étonnés de l'abſurdité de la religion paienne Celle de la religion Papiſte étonnera bien d'avantage un jour la poſterité.—We truſt that day is not

at

ligion very palatable to a voluptuous age, it will not conform its precepts to the standard of fashion; it will not leffen the deformity of vice by lenient appellations; but calls keep-ing, whoredom; intrigue, adultery; and duelling, murder; it will not pander the luft, it will not licenfe the intemperance of mankind; it is a troublefome monitor to a man of pleafure; and your way of life may have made you quarrel with your

at a great diftance, and deifm will then be buried in the ruins of the church of Rome; for the taking the fuperftition, the avarice, the ambi-tion, the intolerance of Antichriftianifm for Chriftianity, has been the great error upon which infidelity has built its fyftem, both at home and abroad.

reli-

religion.—As to your vanity, as a cauſe of your infidelity, ſuffer me to produce the ſentiments of M. Bayle upon that head : if the deſcription does not ſuit your character, you will not be offended at it, and if you are offended with its freedom, it will do you good. "This inclines me to believe, that Libertines, like Des-Barreaux, are not greatly perſuaded of the truth of what they ſay. They have made no deep examination ; they have learned ſome few objections, which they are perpetually making a noiſe with ; they ſpeak from a principle of oſtentation, and give themſelves the lie in the time of danger.—Vanity has a greater ſhare in their diſputes than conſcience, they imagine that the ſingularity and boldneſs of the opi-

5   nions

nions which they maintain, will give them the reputation of men of parts : by degrees, they get a habit of holding impious difcourfes, and if their vanity be accompanied by a voluptuous life, their progrefs in that road is the fwiftei ·."

The main ftrefs of your objections iefts not upon the infufficiency of the external evidence to the truth of Chriftianity ; for few of you, though you may become the future ornaments of the fenate, or of the bar, have ever employed an hour in its examination , but upon the difficulty of the doctrines contained in the New Teftament · they exceed, you fay, your comprehenfion ; and

✝ Bayle, Hift. Dict. Art. Des-Barreaux.

you

you felicitate yourfelves, that you are not yet arrived at the true ftandard of orthodox faith—*credo quia impoffibile.* You think it would be taking a fuperfluous trouble, to enquire into the nature of the external proofs by which Chriftianity is eftablifhed; fince, in your opinion, the book itfelf carries with it its own refutation. A gentleman as acute, probably, as any of you, and who once believed, perhaps, as little as any of you, has drawn a quite different conclufion from the perufal of the New Teftament: his book (however exceptionable it may be thought in fome particular parts) exhibits, not only a diftinguifhed triumph of reafon over prejudice, of Chriftianity over Deifm, but it exhibits, what is infinitely more rare, the character of

a man

a man who has had courage and candour enough to acknowledge it *.

But what if there should be some incomprehensible doctrines in the Christian religion, some circumstances, which in their causes, or their consequences, surpass the reach of human reason; are they to be rejected upon that account? You are, or would be thought, men of reading, and knowledge, and enlarged understandings; weigh the matter fairly; and consider whether revealed religion be not, in this respect, just upon the same footing with every other object of your contemplation. Even in mathematics, the science of demonstration itself, though you get

---

* See A View of the Internal Evidence, &c. by Soame Jenyns,

over

over its firſt principles, and learn to
digeſt the idea of a point without
parts, a line without breadth, and a
ſurface without thickneſs; yet you
will find yourſelf at a loſs to comprehend the perpetual approxima-
tion of lines which can never meet,
the doctrine of incommenſurables,
and of an infinity of infinites, each
infinitely greater, or infinitely leſs,
not only than any finite quanti-
ty, but than each other. In phy-
ſics, you cannot comprehend the primary cauſe of any thing; not of the
light, by which you ſee, nor of the
elaſticity of the air, by which you
hear, nor of the fire, by which you
are warmed. In phyſiology, you
cannot tell what firſt gave motion
to the heart, nor what continues
it; nor why its motion is leſs volun-

rary than that of the lungs ; nor why
you are able to move your arm to
the right or left, by a fimple voli-
tion : you cannot explain the caufe
of animal heat ; nor comprehend the
principle by which your body was at
firft formed, nor by which it is fuf-
tained, nor by which it will be re-
duced to earth. In natural religion,
you cannot comprehend the eternity
or omniprefence of the Deity ; nor
eafily underftand how his prefcience
can be confiftent with your freedom,
or his immutability with his government of moral agents, nor why he
did not make all his creatures equally
perfect ; nor why he did not create
them fooner : in fhort, you cannot
look into any branch of knowledge,
but you will meet with fubjects above
your comprehenfion. The fall and the

redemp-

redemption of human kind are not
more incomprehenfible than the creation and the confervation of the
univerfe, the infinite Author of the
works of providence, and of nature,
is equally infcrutable, equally paft
our finding out in them both. And
it is fomewhat remarkable, that the
deepeft inquirers into nature have
ever thought with moft reverence,
and fpoken with moft diffidence,
concerning thofe things which, in
revealed religion, may feem hard to
be underftood; they have ever avoid-
ed that felf fufficiency of knowledge
which fprings from ignorance, pro-
duces indifference, and ends in infidelity. Admirable to this purpofe,
is the reflection of the greateft ma-
thematician of the prefent age, when
he is combating an opinion of Newton's

ton's by an hypothefis of his own, ftill lefs defenfible than that which he oppofes :—Tous les jours que je vois de ces efprits-forts, qui critique les vérités de notre religion, et s'en mocquent même avec la plus impertinente fuffifance, je penfe, chetifs mortels ! combien et combien des chofes fur lefquelles vous raifonnez fi légèrement, font elles plus fublimes, et plus elévés, que celles fur lefquelles le grand Newton s'égare fi groffièrement *!

Plato mentions a fet of men who were very ignorant, and thought themfelves fupremely wife ; and who rejected the argument for the being of a God, derived from the har-

* Euler.

mony

mony and order of the univerfe, as old and trite *. There have been men, it feems, in all ages, who, in affecting fingularity, have overlooked truth. an argument, however, is not the worfe for being old; and furely it would have been a more juft mode of reafoning, if you had examined the external evidence for the truth of Chriftianity, weighed the old arguments from miracles, and from prophecies, before you had rejected the whole account from the difficulties you met with in it. You would laugh at an Indian, who in peeping into a hiftory of England, and meeting with the mention of the Thames being frozen, or of a fhower of hail, or of fnow, fhould throw the book

* De Leg. lib. x.

aſide.

aside, as unworthy of his further notice, from his want of ability to comprehend these phænomena.

In confidering the argument from
miracles, you will foon be convinced,
that it is poffible for God to work miracles; and you will be convinced,
that it is as poffible for human teftimony to eftablifh the truth of miraculous, as of phyfical or hiftorical
events. but before you can be convinced that the miracles in queftion
are fupported by fuch teftimony as
deferves to be credited, you muft
inquire at what period, and by what
perfons, the books of the Old and
New Teftament were compofed If
you reject the account, without making this examination, you reject it
from prejudice, not from reafon.

There

There is, however, a fhort method of examining this argument, which may, perhaps, make as great an impreffion on your minds as any other. Three men of diftinguifhed abilities rofe up at different times, and attacked Chriftianity with every objection which their malice could fuggeft, or their learning could devife. but neither Celfus in the fecond century, nor Porphyry in the third, nor the emperor Julian himfelf in the fourth century, ever queftioned the reality of the miracles related in the Gofpels. Do but you grant us what thefe men (who were more likely to know the truth of the matter than you can be) granted to their adverfaries, and we will very readily let you make the moft of the Magic, to which, as the laft wretched fhift,

they

they were forced to attribute them. We can find you men, in our days, who, from the mixture of two colourless liquors, will produce you a third as red as blood, or of any other colour you defire ; *et ditto citius*, by a drop refembling water, will reftore the tranfparency, they will make two fluids coalefce into a folid body; and, from the mixture of liquors colder than ice, will inftantly raife you a horrid explofion and a tremendous flame · thefe, and twenty other tricks they will perform, without having been fent with our Saviour to Egypt to learn magic, nay, with a bottle or two of oil, they will compofe the undulations of a lake; and, by a little art, they will reftore the functions of life to a man, who has been an hour or two under water, or

a day

a day or two buried in the fnow : but
in vain will thefe men, or the greateft
magician that Egypt ever faw, fay to
a boifterous fea, *Peace, be ftill*; in
vain will they fay to a carcafe rotting
in the grave, *Come forth* · the winds
and the fea will not obey them, and
the putrid carcafe will not hear them
You need not fuffer yourfelves to be
deprived of the weight of this argument, from its having been obferved, that the Fathers have acknowledged the fupernatural part of
Paganifm ; fince the Fathers were in
no condition to detect a cheat, which
was fupported both by the difpofition of the people, and the power
of the civil magiftrate *, and they
were from that inability forced to

attribute to infernal agency, what
was too cunningly contrived to be
detected, and contrived for too impious a purpose, to be credited as
the work of God.

With refpect to prophecy, you
may, perhaps, have accuftomed yourfelves to confider it as originating in
Afiatic enthufiafm, in Chaldean myftery, or in the fubtle ftratagem of
interefted Priefts, and have given
yourfelves no more trouble concerning the predictions of facred, than
concerning the oracles of Pagan hiftory. Or if you have ever caft a
glance upon this fubject, the diffen-
fons of learned men concerning the
proper interpretation of the Revc-
lation, and other difficult prophecies, may have made you rafhly

con-

conclude, that all prophecies were equally unintelligible, and more in-debted for their accomplishment to a fortunate concurrence of events, and the pliant ingenuity of the expositor, than to the infpired forefight of the prophet. In all that the prophets of the Old Teftament have delivered, concerning the de-ftruction of particular cities, and the defolation of particular kingdoms, you may fee nothing but fhrewd con-jectures, which any one acquainted with the hiftory of the rife and fall of empires might certainly have made; and as you would not hold him for a prophet, who fhould not affirm, that London or Paris would afford to future ages a fpectacle juft as melancholy as that which we now contemplate, with a figh, in the ruins

ruins of Agrigentum or Palmyra, fo
you cannot perfuade yourfelves to
believe that the denunciations of
the prophets againft tne haughty cities of Tyre or Babylon, for inftance,
proceeded from the infpiration of
the Deity. There is no doubt, that
by fome fuch general kind of reafoning, many are influenced to pay
no attention to an argument, which,
if properly confidered, carries with
it the ftrongeft conviction.

Spinoza faid, That he would have
broken his atheiftic fyftem to pieces,
and embraced without repugnance
the ordinary faith of Chriftians, if he
could have perfuaded himfelf of the
refurrection of Lazarus from the
dead; and I queftion not, that there
are many difbelievers who would re-

linquifh

linquish their Deiftic tenets, and receive the gofpel, if they could perfuade themfelves, that God had ever fo far interfered in the moral government of the world, as to illumine the mind of any one man with the knowledge of future events. A miracle ftrikes the fenfes of the perfons who fee it ; a prophecy addreffes itfelf to the underftandings of thofe who behold its completion ; and it requires, in many cafes, fome learning, in all fome attention, to judge of the correfpondence of events with the predictions concerning them. No one can be convinced, that what Jeremiah and the other prophets foretold of the fate of Babylon, that it fhould be befieged by the Medes, that it fhould be taken, when her mighty men were drunken, when her

fprings

fprings were dried up; and that it fhould become a pool of water, and fhould remain defolate for ever, no one, I fay, can be convinced, that all thefe, and other parts of the prophetic denunciation, have been minutely fulfilled, without fpending fome time in reading the accounts which profane hiftorians have delivered down to us concerning its being taken by Cyrus, and which modern travellers have given us of its prefent fituation.

Porphyry was fo perfuaded of the coincidence between the prophecies of Daniel and the events, that he was forced to affirm, the prophecies were written after the things prophefied of had happened. Another Porphyry has, in our days, been fo afto-

L 4

nifhed

aſhed at the correſpondence between the prophecy concerning the deſtruction of Jeruſalem, as related by St. Matthew, and the hiſtory of that event, as recorded by Joſephus, that, rather than embrace Chriſtianity, he has ventured (contrary to the faith of all eccleſiaſtical hiſtory, the opinion of the learned of all ages, and all the rules of good criticiſm) to aſſert, that St. Matthew wrote his Goſpel after Jeruſalem had been taken and deſtroyed by the Romans. You may from theſe inſtances perceive the ſtrength of the argument from prophecy ; it has not been able indeed to vanquiſh the prejudices of either the ancient or the modern Porphyry, but it has been able to compel them both to be guilty of obvious falſehoods, which have nothing

thing but impudent affertions to fupport them.

Some over-zealous interpreters of
fcripture have found prophecies in
fimple narrations, extended real predictions beyond the times and circumftances to which they naturally
were applied, and perplexed their
readers with a thoufand quaint allu-
fions and allegorical conceits. this
proceeding has made men of fenfe
pay lefs regard to prophecy in general. There are fome predictions,
however, fuch as thofe concerning
the prefent ftate of the Jewifh people, and the corruption of Chriftianity, which are now fulfilling in
the world; and which, if you will
take the trouble to examine them,
you will find of fuch an extraordi-

L 5   nary

nary nature, that you will not perhaps hefitate'to refer them to God
as their author, and if you once become perfuaded of the truth of any
one miracle, or of the completion of
any one prophecy, you will refolve
all your difficulties (concerning the
manner of God's interpofition in
the moral government of our fpecies, and the nature of the doctrines
contained in revelation) into your
own inability fully to comprehend
the whole fcheme of divine Providence.

We are told, however, that the
ftrangenefs of the narration, and the
difficulty of the doctrines contained
in the New Teftament, are not the
only circumftances which induce you
to reject it; you have difcovered,

you think, fo many contradictions in
the accounts which the Evangelifts
have given of the life of Chrift, that
you are compelled to confider the
whole as an ill-digefted and improbable ftory. You would not reafon
thus upon any other occafion; you
would not reject as fabulous the accounts given by Livy and Polybius
of Hannibal and the Carthaginians,
though you fhould difcover a difference betwixt them in feveral
points of little importance. You
cannot compare the hiftory of the
fame events as delivered by any
two hiftorians, but you will meet with
many circumftances, which, though
mentioned by one, are either wholly
omitted, or differently related by the
other, and this obfervation is peculiarly applicable to biographical writ-

L 6

ings : but no one ever thought of difbelieving the leading circumftances of the lives of Vitellius or Vefpafian, becaufe Tacitus and Suetonius did not in every thing correfpond in their accounts of thefe emperors. And if the memoirs of the life and doctrines of M. de Voltaire himfelf were, fome twenty or thirty years after his death, to be delivered to the world by four of his moft intimate acquaintance, I do not apprehend that we fhould difcredit the whole account of fuch an extraordinary man, by reafon of fome flight inconfiftencies and contradictions which the avowed enemies of his name might chance to difcover in the feveral narrations. Though we fhould grant you then, that the Evangelifts had fallen into fome trivial contradictions,

dictions, in what they have related concerning the life of Chrift; yet you ought not to draw any other inference from our conceffion than that they had not plotted together, as cheats would have done, in order to give an unexceptionable confiftency to their fraud. We are not however difpofed to make you any fuch conceffion, we will rather fhew you the futility of your general argument, by touching upon a few of the places which you think are moft liable to your cenfure.

You obferve, that neither Luke, nor Mark, nor John have mentioned the cruelty of Herod in murdering the infants of Bethlehem, and that no account is to be found of this matter in Jofephus, who wrote the
life

life of Herod ; and therefore the fact recorded by Matthew is not true. —The concurrent teſtimony of many independent writers concerning a matter of fact unqueſtionably adds to its probability; but if nothing is to be received as true, upon the teſti- mony of a ſingle author, we muſt give up ſome of the beſt writers, and diſbelieve ſome of the moſt intereſt- ing facts of ancient hiſtory.

According to Matthew, Mark, and Luke, there was only an interval of three months, you ſay, between the baptiſm and crucifixion of Jeſus, from which time, taking away the forty days of the temptation, there will only remain about ſix weeks for the whole period of his public miniſtry; which laſted however, according

cording to St. John, at the leaft
above three years.—Your objection
fairly ftated ftands thus. Matthew,
Mark, and Luke, in writing the hiftory of Jefus Chrift, mention the feveral events of his life, as following
one another in continued fucceffion,
without taking notice of the times
in which they happened : but is it a
juft conclufion from their filence, to
infer that there really were no inter-
vals of time between the tranfactions
which they feem to have connected ?
Many inftances might be produced
from the moft admired biographers
of antiquity, in which events are related, as immediately confequent to
each other, which did not happen
but at very diftant periods . we have
an obvious example of this manner
of writing in St. Matthew; who con-

nects

nects the preaching of John the Baptift with the return of Jofeph from Egypt, though we are certain that the latter event preceded the former by a great many years.

John has faid nothing of the inftitution of the Lord's fupper, the other Evangelifts have faid nothing of the wafhing of the difciples' feet. —What then ? are you not afhamed to produce thefe facts, as inftances of contradiction ? If omiffions are contradictions, look into the hiftory of the age of Louis the Fourteenth, or into the general hiftory of M. de Voltaire, and you will meet with a great abundance of contradictions.

John, in mentioning the difcourfe which Jefus had with his mother and his

his beloved difciple, at the time of his crucifixion, fays, that fhe with Mary Magdalene ftood near the crofs. Matthew, on the other hand, fays, that Mary Magdalene and the other women were there, beholding afar off. This you think a manifeft contradiction, and fcoffingly inquire, whether the women and the beloved difciple, which were near the crofs, could be the fame with thofe who ftood far from the crofs?—It is difficult not to tranfgrefs the bounds of moderation and good manners, in anfwering fuch fophiftry. What! have you to learn, that though the Evangelifts fpeak of the crucifixion as of one event, it was not accomplifhed in one inftant, but lafted feveral hours? And why the women, who were at a diftance from the crofs, might not, during its continuance, draw near

the

the crofs; or, from being near the crofs, might not move from the crofs, is more than you can explain to either us or yourfelves. And we take from you your only refuge, by denying exprefsly, that the different Evangelifts, in their mention of the women, fpeak of the fame point of time.

The Evangelifts, you affirm, are fallen into grofs contradictions, in their accounts of the appearances by which Jefus manifefted himfelf to his difciples, after his refurrection from the dead; for Matthew fpeaks of two, Mark of three, Luke of two, and John of four. That contradictory propofitions cannot be true, is readily granted; and if you will produce the place in which Matthew

fays,

fays, that Jefus Chrift appeared twice
and *no oftener*, it will be further
granted, that he is contradicted by
John in a very material part of his
narration. but till you do that, you
muft excufe me, if I cannot grant,
that the Evangelifts have contradicted each other in this point, for
to common underftandings it is pretty
evident, that if Chrift appeared four
times, according to John's account,
he muft have appeared twice, according to that of Matthew and
Luke, and thrice, according to that
of Mark.

The different Evangelifts are not
only accufed of contradicting each
other, but Luke is faid to have contradicted himfelf; for in his Gofpel
he tells us, that Jefus afcended into

heaven

heaven from Bethany, and in the Acts of the Apoftles, of which he is the reputed author, he informs us that he afcended from Mount Olivet. —Your objection proceeds either from your ignorance of geography, or your ill-will to Chriftianity, and upon either fuppofition deferves our contempt: be pleafed, however, to remember for the future, that Bethany was not only the name of a town, but of a diftrict of Mount Olivet adjoining to the town.

From this fpecimen of the contradictions afcribed to the hiftorians of the life of Chrift, you may judge for yourfelves what little reafon there is to reject Chriftianity upon their account; and how fadly you will be impofed upon (in a matter of more confe-

consequence to you than any other)
if you take every thing for a contradiction, which the uncandid adver-
saries of Christianity think proper to
call one.

Before I put an end to this address,
I cannot help taking notice of an
argument by which some philosophers have of late endeavoured to
overturn the whole system of revelation; and it is the more necessary
to give an answer to their objection,
as it is become a common subject of
philosophical conversation, especially
amongst those who have visited the
continent. The objection tends to
invalidate, as is supposed, the authority of Moses, by shewing that the
earth is much older than it can be
proved to be from his account of the

creation,

creation, and the fcripture chrono-
logy. We contend, that fix thoufand years have not yet elapfed fince
the creation ; and thefe philofophers
contend, that they have indubitable
proof of the earth's being at the leaft
fourteen thoufand years old ; and they
complain that Mofes hangs as a
dead weight upon them, and blunts
all their zeal for inquiry *.

The Canonico Recupero, who, it
feems, is engaged in writing the hif
tory of mount Etna, has difcovered
a ftratum of lava which flowed from
that mountain, according to his opinion, in the time of the fecond Pu-
nic war, or about two thoufand years
ago, this ftratum is not yet covered

* Brydone's Travels.

with

7

with foil fufficient for the production
of either corn or vines; it requires
then, fays the Canon, two thoufand
years at leaft to convert a ftratum of
lava into a fertile field. In finking
a pit near *Jaci*, in the neighbourhood
of Etna, they have difcovered evident marks of feven diftinct lavas
one under the other ; the furfaces of
which are parallel, and moft of them
covered with a thick bed of rich
earth : now, the eruption which
formed the loweft of thefe lavas (if
we may be allowed to reafon, fays
the Canon, from analogy) flowed
from the mountain at leaft fourteen
thoufand years ago.——It might be
briefly anfwered to this objection,
by denying that there is any thing
in the hiftory of Mofes repugnant
to this opinion concerning the great

anti-

antiquity of the earth; for though
the rife and progress of arts and
fciences, and the fmall multiplication
of the human fpecies, render it almoft to a demonftration probable,
that man has not exifted longer upon
the furface of this earth than according to the Mofaic account; yet that
the earth itfelf was then created out
of nothing, when man was placed
upon it, is not, according to the fen-
timents of fome philofophers, to be
proved from the original text of facred fcripture. we might, I fay, reply with thefe philofophers to this
formidable objection of the Canon,
by granting it in its full extent, we
are under no neceffity, however, of
adopting their opinion in order to
fhew the weaknefs of the Canon's reafoning. For, in the firft place, the

Canon has not fatisfactorily eftablifhed his main fact, that the lava
in queftion is the identical lava which
Diodorus Siculus mentions to have
flowed from Etna, in the fecond Car-
thaginian war; and in the fecond
place it may be obferved, that the
time neceffary for converting lavas
into fertile fields muft be very different, according to the different con-
fiftencies of the lavas, and their different fituations, with refpect to ele-
vation or depreffion ; to their being
expofed to winds, rains, and to other
circumftances ; juft as the time in
which the heaps of iron flag (which
refembles lava) are covered with
verdure, is different at different fur-
naces, according to the nature of the
flag, and fituation of the furnace;
and fomething of this kind is dedu-

M   cible

cible from the account of the Canon himfelf, fince the crevices of this famous ftratum are really full of rich, good foil, and have pretty large trees growing in them.

But if all this fhould be thought not fufficient to remove the objection, I will produce the Canon an analogy in oppofition to his analogy, and which is grounded on more certain facts. Etna and Vefuvius refemble each other, in the caufes which produce their eruptions, and in the nature of their lavas, and in the time neceffary to mellow them into foil fit for vegetation; or if there be any flight difference in this refpect, it is probably not greater than what fubfifts between different lavas of the fame mountain. This being

admit-

admitted, which no philosopher will deny, the Canon's analogy will prove just nothing at all, if we can produce an instance of seven different lavas (with interjacent strata of vegetable earth) which have flowed from mount Vesuvius, within the space, not of fourteen thousand, but of somewhat less than seventeen hundred years, for then, according to our analogy, a stratum of lava may be covered with vegetable soil in about two hundred and fifty years, instead of requiring two thousand for the purpose. The eruption of Vesuvius, which destroyed Herculaneum and Pompeii, is rendered still more famous by the death of Pliny, recorded by his nephew in his letter to Tacitus, this event happened in the year 79, it is not yet then quite

seven-

feventeen hundred years fince Herculaneum was fwallowed up . but
we are informed by unqueftionable
authority, that " the matter which
covers the ancient town of Herculaneum is not the produce of one
eruption only ; for there are evident
marks, that the matter of fix eruptions has taken its courfe over that
which lies immediately above the
town, and was the caufe of its de-
ftruction. Thefe ftrata are either of
lava or burnt matter, *with veins of
good foil betwixt them* ."—I will not
add another word upon this fubject ;
except that the bifhop of the diocefe

* See Sir William Hamilton's Remarks
upon the Nature of the Soil of Naples and its
Neighbourhood, in the Philof. Tranf. vol. lxi.
p. 7.

was not much out in his advice to Canonico Recupeio—to take care not
to make his mountain older than
Mofes; though it would have been
full as well to have fhut his mouth
with a reafon, as to have ftopped it
with the dread of an ecclefiaftical
cenfure.

You perceive with what eafe a
little attention will remove a great
difficulty; but had we been able to
fay nothing in explanation of this
phænomenon, we fhould not have
acted a very rational part in making
our ignorance the foundation of our
infidelity, or fuffering a minute philofopher to rob us of our religion.

Your objections to revelation may
be numerous; you may find fault

with

with the account which Mofes has given of the creation and the fall, you may not be able to get water enough for an univerfal deluge, nor room enough in the ark of Noah for all the different kinds of aerial and terreftrial animals; you may be dif-fatisfied with the command for fa-crificing of Ifaac, for plundering the Egyptians, and for extirpating the Canaanites; you may find fault with the Jewifh œconomy, for its cere-monies, its facrifices, and its multi-plicity of priefts; you may object to the imprecations in the Pfalms, and think the immoralities of David a fit fubject for dramatic ridicule [*],

you

---

[*] See Saül et David Hyperdrame.

Whatever cenfure the author of this compo-fition

8

you may look upon the partial pro-
mulgation of Chriſtianity as an inſu-
perable objection to its truth, and
waywardly reject the goodneſs of
God toward yourſelves, becauſe you
do not comprehend how you have
deſerved it more than others, you
may know nothing of the entrance
of ſin and death into the world by
one man's tranſgreſſion ; nor be able
to comprehend the doctrine of the
croſs and of redemption by Jeſus
Chriſt, in ſhort, if your mind is ſo
diſpoſed, you may find food for your
ſcepticiſm in every page of the Bible,
as well as in every appearance of nature, and it is not in the power of

fition may deſerve for his intention, the work
itſelf deſerves none, its ridicule is too groſs to
miſlead even the ignorant.

any

any perfon, but yourfelves, to clear
up your doubts; you muft read, and
you muft think for yourfelves ; and
you muft do both with temper, with
candour, and with care. Infidelity
is a rank weed, it is nurtured by
our vices, and cannot be plucked up
as eafily as it may be planted   your
difficulties with refpect to revelation
may have firft arifen from your own
reflection on the religious indifference of thofe, whom, from your
earlieft infancy, you have been accuftomed to revere and imitate, do-
meftic irreligion may have made you
a willing hearer of libertine converfation ; and the uniform prejudices
of the world may have finifhed the
bufinefs, at a very early age, and left
you to wander through life, without
a principle to direct your conduct,
                                    and

and to die without hope. We are
far from wifhing you to truft the
word of the Clergy for the truth of
your religion ; we beg of you to
examine it to the bottom, to try it, to
prove it, and not to hold it faft unlefs you find it good. Till you are
difpofed to undertake this tafk, it becomes you to confider with great
ferioufnefs and attention, whether it
can be for your intereft to efteem a
few witty farcafms, or metaphyfic
fubtleties, or ignorant mifreprefen-
tations, or unwarranted affertions, as
unanfwerable arguments againft revelation ; and a very flight reflection
will convince you, that it will certainly be for your reputation to em-
ploy the flippancy of your rhetoric,
and the poignancy of your ridicule,

upon

upon any subject rather than upon
the subject of Religion.

I take my leave with recommending to your notice, the advice which
Mr. Locke gave to a young man
who was desirous of becoming acquainted with the doctrines of the
Christian religion.—" Study the holy
scripture, especially the New Testa-
ment : therein are contained the
words of eternal life. It has God
for its author, salvation for its end,
and truth without any mixture of
error for its matter *."

I am, &c.

* Locke's Posth. Works.

FINIS.

Lightning Source UK Ltd.
Milton Keynes UK
UKHW031232200521
384060UK00006B/967